COVENANT CHILDBIRTH

SPIRITUAL HOPE FOR EXPECTANT MOTHERS AND FAMILIES STRUGGLING WITH CHILDBIRTH

CALLISTUS IKE

Published by KHARIS PUBLISHING, an imprint of
KHARIS MEDIA LLC

Copyright © 2016 Callistus Ike

ISBN-13: 978-1-946277-02-2
ISBN: 10: 1-946277-02-9

Unless otherwise stated, all scriptural quotations are from the
King James Version (KJV)

All KHARIS PUBLISHING products are available at special
quantity discounts for bulk purchase for sales promotions,
premiums, fund-raising, and educational needs. For details, write:

Kharis Media LLC
709 SW Elmside Drive
Bentonville,
AR 72712
Tel: 479-903-8160
info@kharispublishing.com
www.kharispublishing.com

DEDICATION

Unto Him that loved us,
And washed us in His own blood,
And has made us kings and priest unto God and His Father;
To Him be glory and dominion for ever and ever. Amen!
(Rev. 1:5-6)

CONTENTS

ACKNOWLEDGMENTS

Appreciation to my wife who, through faith and patience, has proven with me the principles outlined in this book.

PREFACE

Fruitfulness is a covenant! As a covenant, it was not the idea of man but was established by an unchanging decree from the Almighty. The Lord says, in Psalm 89:34, "My covenant will I not break, nor alter the thing that is gone out of my lips." He continues in Psalm 113:9 by saying that he "maketh the barren woman to keep house and to be a joyful mother of children. Praise ye the Lord."

You see, it doesn't matter how precarious your case may seem to be; His word must surely come to pass in your life. Satan does not have the final say. Medical diagnoses and laboratory reports do not have finality either. No, let us "fear God and keep his commandments; for this is the whole duty of man" (Eccl. 12:13).

Until God concludes a matter, no man can successfully give the final verdict. Because with God, nothing is impossible (Lk. 1:37). Until God says it's over, it is not really over. I know that He has changed uteri and replaced fallopian tubes in order to protect the integrity of His word. I know that He has raised sperm counts (whether they were nonexistent, low, or something in between) and rectified watery sperm so as to bring His word to pass.

This same God has uprooted fibroids and all forms of

negative conditions, whether physical or spiritual, in order to bring about the fulfillment of His word because, as He says in Job 28:9, "He putteth forth His hand upon the rock; He over turneth the mountains by the root." No matter how rocky or hard you think your situation is, we have a God who is a specialist at uprooting the difficult situations of life, so "weep not; behold, the lion of the tribe of Judah has prevailed" (Rev. 5:5).

If there is a person to believe, there is a God to perform! Even if you seem not to have any physical capacity for pregnancy, God is more than able to grace you with the ability to procreate. When God qualifies you, nothing can disqualify you. Your condition can not intimidate the Almighty! You are just at the right place for a miracle.

This book is dedicated with prayers and thanksgiving for the joy of your family. I know that most of you reading this book now will be carrying your baby in the womb before you read the last sentence of this book.

As you absorb the truth embedded in this book, whether in the course of reading the book or after, the truth remains that you cannot be denied. As it says in the Bible, "He that spared not His own son, but delivered Him up for us all, how shall He not with Him also freely give us all things?" (Rom. 8:32).

Don't be taken unawares. Please start shopping for your nursing items and don't you ever forget to send me an invitation card for your child's dedication.

Wipe those tears away, for now I know that you shall have your babies. Welcome to the world of parenthood in Jesus' precious name!

Before you go any further in this book, I suggest that you pause here and make a commitment of your life to Jesus, who is the reason for all these blessings. He purchased us all with His blood, and I do believe you can experience salvation now through a simple faith in Him.

Let's pray this prayer aloud together:

Father, I thank you for sending Jesus to die in my place. I believe that His blood has washed my sins away. I confess Jesus as the Lord of my life, and I do believe in my heart that God raised Him from the dead for my redemption. Thank you Father for saving me. Amen. I am now born again; now I am a child of God. Amen!

If you have just done that, ask God to direct you to a church where you will serve and know more about Him, if you are not already in one. Just as a tree needs the soil to grow, you will need your church family to grow in the Lord.

If you are looking up to God for a baby or babies, I do encourage you not to read this book as you would read your novel. Rather, take out time and *study* this book, going through all the Bible references. If it is important to you, you must find time to be *alone* with God. Great things happen when you give Him your total and undivided attention.

1 PREVAILING TRUTH

And you shall know the truth and the truth shall make you free (Jn. 8:32)
Sanctify them through thy truth, thy word is truth (Jn. 17:17)

The truth of the word of God is superior to circumstantial evidences. The truth we are about to unfold here by the Holy Spirit is so tremendous that you will conceive by it. The reason a woman takes in is not just because a man's sperm fertilizes the ova but because the Almighty has decreed: "Be fruitful and multiply!" (Gen. 1:28).

The force that releases the ova in the woman and the sperm from the man (and the subsequent fertilization) is in obedience to this eternal decree. The ova and the sperm are physical things, but your baby is a spirit being wearing an earthly body. It is absolutely impossible for the physical to give birth to the spiritual. Your baby is a gift from God, not a result of biological conjugation. Sex is very important, but it is only God's insignia and imprimatur on the sacred institution of marriage. Does this nullify sex? No! Rather, sex within the confines of marriage is the means to the ends of procreation.

The word of God is the womb of creation. What does that translate to? Your fruitfulness is not based on your doctor's conclusions derived from a medical diagnosis. Your fruitfulness is rooted in the integrity of the everlasting God who has said to you: Be fruitful and multiply. Everything He commanded to **be** became whatever He decreed them to be. For you to know that He is referring to you personally, He says: "And you [fit in your name here], be fruitful, and multiply; bring forth abundantly in the earth, and multiply therein" (Gen. 9:7).

Stop celebrating those negative doctors' reports. We are not contesting what the doctors claimed to have seen, but we know that until a man sees things from God's own perspective, he has not really seen well. In as much as you are encouraged to get all the medical assistance you may require, we still insist that you must not accept any negative or hopeless reports.

Oftentimes, what they call hopeless or terminal are other ways of advertising the limitations of medical science. This is by no means an indictment on the medical profession, since I encourage couples to go and get a medical test. Rather, it's always been a good clue in knowing where the devil is trying to tell another lie.

Every lie that the devil has sold to you as touching your ability to carry your baby stands destroyed now in Jesus' name.

Your conception and eventual delivery is a non-negotiable truth, no matter what the devil has stolen or implanted in your body.

The best that the devil does is to tell lies against God, against you and your body, and even against your spouse. The truth is the opposite of whatever the devil has told you. When Adam said to God, "we heard your voice and we hid ourselves because we were naked", God asked them, "Who told you?" (Gen. 3:10-11). God asked this even though He knew it was the devil.

Concerning the negative reports you are parading about and which have also stifled your faith, the question is, who told you that? If God did not say that to you, then rejoice "for there is hope of a tree if it be cut down, that it will sprout again" (Job 14:7). God hopes to "sanctify and cleanse [you] with the washing of water by the word" (Eph. 5:26).

Through the scent of the water of the word of God, you shall be fruitful; I hear the sound of rejoicing in your home again. Your past experiences will not stop your miracle and joy.

You **shall** bring forth your babies in Jesus' name for "He maketh the barren woman to keep house, and to be a joyful mother of children" (Ps. 113: 9).

God will renew your age and heal whatever that has died in you and make you, through the power of the Holy Ghost, bring forth children like a young lady in Jesus' name!

You are a tree of righteousness! You are the planting of the Lord! You are planted in a most fruitful hill. You are abundantly fruitful. You are not trying to be, *you are already*! If you believe, you will see it happen without delays. You will see that "blessed is she that believeth; for there shall be a performance of those things which were told her from the Lord" (Lk. 1:45).

I am not unmindful of those private tears and disappointments whenever you see your monthly period. God has a different agenda for you. He has commissioned this book in order to, "appoint unto them that mourn in Zion, to give unto them beauty for ashes, the oil of joy for mourning, the garment of praise for the spirit of heaviness, that they might be called the trees of righteousness, the planting of the Lord, that He might be glorified" (Isa. 61:3).

The purpose of God for His children cannot be defeated if they walk in the light of His revealed word. You shall not miss out on your covenant right in Jesus' name!

Was it Papa Abraham's sperm that produced Isaac? The Lord returned to overrule barrenness. He came back to fulfill His word! Sperm or no sperm, Isaac was born because the word of God is far too precious and powerful to be left at the mercy of such a biological fluid called sperm. As soon as it was time, His eternal presence took over and his sperm were rejuvenated; the end product was the result of Abraham's faith.

Sperm, ovaries, fallopian tubes and the entire process of conception and delivery are all dependent on the integrity of the infallible word of God.

It doesn't matter what the devil has stolen from your body, God will replace it, repair it, or give you your babies without it.

The wisdom of God far outweighs the calculations of medical science in its entirety. You are not barren; you are a fruitful mother of children. Get set and prepare for them now. Go and carefully pick your nursing items.

You are not infertile; you are a joyful father of children. Start planning for their birth, education and general upbringing now for "about this season, according to the time of life, you shall embrace your baby in Jesus' name! (2 Kings 4:16).

The word of God is the womb of creation.

Abraham's body was dead; Sarah's womb was dead, so how did Isaac come about?

God decreed it when he said, "Sarah thy wife shall have a son!" (Gen. 18:10)

And what Jesus has said, He says unto you all (Mk. 13:37).

It was not a suggestion; it was an eternal decree that proceeded from the lips of the father of all creation.

Was the birth of Isaac a mere result of a conjugal relationship? Far from the truth! Listen to these sweet words: "Through faith also Sara herself received strength to conceive seed, and was delivered of a child when she was past age, because she judged Him faithful who had promised" (Heb. 11:11).

Sarah received strength to conceive. You too shall

receive strength to conceive today in Jesus' name!

Sarah took in and delivered Isaac because God returned to fulfill His word. God returned and Isaac was born. He returned because "she judged Him faithful who had promised" (Heb. 11:11).

We can provoke His return by walking in faith. Through faith, Sarah received strength to conceive. The strength to conceive is already available for you, paid for by Jesus, and waiting for you to step out and receive it in faith.

Another witness I wish to call up is the Shunamite woman. She had no child, in spite of all she and her husband did, until the word of the Lord came to her through His prophet Elisha, saying, "About this season according to the time of life thou shall embrace a son" (2 Kings 4:16).

It was a royal decree with all the finality of an imperial order. It neither had respect for the couple's age nor for the condition of their reproductive systems. It's the word of God on mission, and it can neither return empty nor voided. The prosperity of the word must be established. The decreed son must be produced, negative biological evidences notwithstanding. "And the woman conceived, and bore a son at that season that Elisha had said unto her, according to the time of life" (2 Kings 4:17).

It's now your turn! You are next in line!

The next witnesses I wish to call up are the parents of Samson, Manoah and his wife, because: "in the mouth of two or three witnesses, every word shall be established" (2 Cor. 13:1).

Manoah and his wife were barren and without children. But then, the angel of the Lord appeared to the woman and said to her that though she is "barren and ha[s] no children, but you shall become pregnant and bear a son" (Judg. 13:2-3).

God sent a messenger with a message of supernatural conception to this family. They received his message, believed him and acted on it. The rest, they say, is not just history but a landmark of faith.

The same God has sent me to you with the same message of supernatural conception. You have a choice to do just like they did. Either you can believe His message for you and follow through with the instructions being outlined for you in this book, or you can allow your experiences, people's opinions, and 'expert' advice, which may seem and sound valid, talk you out of the arena of faith and into the "common sense" of man.

May God Himself talk some real faith into us through His word!

The barren womb of Manoah's wife could not resist the message of procreation from the messenger of God. God had said: but you shall become pregnant and bear a son! Don't miss a good place to say amen. Hallelujah!

God said to her, I know your situation **but**, I know the medical records **but**, I know the diagnosis **but**, I know how long it's been **but**, I know the way you feel **but**, I know what the neighbors and in-laws are saying **but**, I know the dark secrets, *but* you shall become pregnant and carry the baby of your choice!

God planted His word into the soil of her supposedly barren womb, and the woman bore a son and called him Samson, "and the child grew and the Lord blessed him" (Judg. 13:24).

What would you call your baby?

You don't know the reason why I speak the way I do. When a man has heard from God and has seen Him confirm it over and over in real life situations, he speaks with undying confidence. Not only has He done it in our lives, we've seen Him replicate it again and again in the lives of the people we have ministered to.

Some years back, we had a neighbor whose wife had two beautiful daughters. This couple and their kids love us so much. One day, years into our relationship, the Lord told me to ask her if she wouldn't like to have another baby. I confided in my wife, who encouraged me to ask her as I was directed by the lord.

When I eventually asked her, she opened a can of worms, details of which I cannot divulge, but I told her that God knew all about that and still wanted to bless her. I led her in a prayer of repentance and confession and later placed her on a few days of fasting, after which I asked her to return for us to pray with her.

A few weeks after these prayers, she took in and later gave birth to a bouncing baby boy. I stand in awe of God for who He is and for what He can do! He will do that in your life and family in Jesus' precious name!

Some time back, while lodging at my friend's place during one of my visits to Lagos, I asked him whether they were deliberately practicing family planning or something else. You know, you can be blunt with your friends sometimes. He laughed and told me that the absence of children in the house was not due to any form of family planning but rather that they were eagerly expecting to have theirs as well. When I spoke with his wife, her faith was red hot to receive from God.

Before I left Lagos, I had a prayer session with the couple, after which I told them that they must meet that same day as couples do. I didn't know why but that was what God impressed on my heart, and I'm glad they obeyed! Shortly after that, I got a call from the wife that she just had a positive pregnancy test and that the date of conception was precisely the same day that they received the prayers and instruction. Today, they are parents to three wonderful children. To God be all the glory!

Once, after ministering in a vigil at one of the Assemblies of God churches in the former Lagos district, a woman invited us to her home for a breakfast where she sumptuously fed us. After the meal, she asked us to pray for her conception. The service she rendered to us was a voice that could not be resisted. A few months after the prayer, she took in and subsequently gave birth to a bouncing baby boy. She literally drew virtue out of us.

While I was still in Bible School, we had an encounter

with a Muslim woman who had been childless during her thirteen years of marriage. She invited us through one of our colleagues to come pray for her. After ministering the word and prayer of faith to her, God broke thirteen years of barrenness. She had a beautiful baby girl.

Fruitfulness is so important to God that He would not abandon it to changing biological situations.

God has purposed that you shall be fruitful, because it pleases Him (Gen. 1:28).

Since everything in creation produces after its kind by the word of creation and on the same breath God uttered his decree of fruitfulness, I submit that no obstruction in the process of human procreation has the right to stop that order in your life.

Your business is to do your part: Believe! Jesus said, "If you can believe, all things are possible" (Mk. 9:23).

The Lord has said, "There shall nothing cast their young, nor be barren in thy land" (Ex. 23:26). Do you believe this?

He has already said that He will love, bless, and multiply you. Do you believe this?

He has even said in Deuteronomy 7 that, "there shall not be mall or female barren among you, or among your cattle."

You know what that means? Not even your pets or anything around you is permitted to be barren. So then, how much more you? Barrenness is not permitted to survive around you. You are a threat to barrenness. You are a life carrier. The force of procreation is already at work on your insides. I see your baby kicking on your inside! I see you carrying your baby! I see people gathering to celebrate with you and your family.

Believe and maintain an attitude of praise and thanksgiving. We don't need to teach Him how to do His part. Speak truth over your neighbors and give good to them, without withholding, as it says in Proverbs 3:27. Help them remember that "children are a heritage of the Lord and the fruit of the womb is His reward" (Ps. 127:3). Nothing is ever wrong from God's own end. We must constantly cross check our own end here.

The Lord is good and gives good things. "How much more shall your father which is in heaven give good things to them that ask Him" (Matt. 7:11).

You are next in line!!!

2 CALLING FORTH THE INVISIBLE

...before Him whom he believed, even God, who quickeneth the dead, and calleth those things which be not as though they were (Rom. 4:17)

Your faith in God's ability will make all the difference in your life. Abraham believed in the God who gives life to the dead and speaks of the nonexistent things as if they already exist. That is the language of faith.

Please notice that He speaks of his children that were not yet born as though they were already living with him right there. Can you beat that?

As a parent, even when your child is not present in the same room with you, he still exists elsewhere. As long as he hears your voice, he is bound to answer you. It sounds and seems preposterous if you conclude that you don't have a child based on the medical facts that you have.

God doesn't wait for the medical reports to be okay; He says none shall be barren nor miscarry. He makes the barren to conceive and become a joyful mother of children. He doesn't need any medical confirmation to bring His word to pass in your life. Just believe Him. The foolishness of God is still wiser than men, according to 1 Corinthians 1:25.

Under the cultural context in which we live, even if your child is out of ear shot, people will help you in calling him. This is why the ministers of the gospel and other believers who share your faith in God's ability can help you in calling children forth in prayers of agreement. That was what Eli did for Hannah. That was what Elisha did for the Shunamite woman. That was what the Angel did for Manoah's wife. That is what I am doing for you right now. Be fruitful in Jesus' name!!!

Your child pre-existed before God ever laid the foundation of the world (Eph. 1:4). That was why God could say to Jeremiah: "Before I formed thee in the belly I knew thee" (Jer. 1:5). You are not calling a non-existent child, you are calling for your child that is already waiting for your call.

If there are things dead or inoperative in your life, whether sperm, womb, blocked fallopian tubes or whatsoever it is, He will give life to the dead or inoperative organs.

Whatever that is blocked in you is unblocked now in Jesus' name!

Whatever that is lacking in your system is filled up now by the supply of the spirit in Jesus' name!

Nothing intimidates God; rather, the challenges of life are His opportunities to display His awesome power in your life and family. He is "a very present help in trouble" (Ps. 46:1).

In the school of faith, calling forth the invisible is the Headmaster. You must keep speaking the truth of the word of God because "we walk by faith and not by sight" (2 Cor. 5:7).

In the school of faith, we trade with the word of God. That is the reason He says we should take our minds off what we can see and, through His word, keep calling those things that we desire but are not present now in our lives, be they babies or any other thing. The children are bound to answer! His word in our mouths is the master of situations. It will never lack its material equivalent, for we are told in Isaiah 34 that not one detail of prophecy shall fail.

Keep speaking the word. His word is the incubator of life!

When you seek out the mind of God from His book, believe it and keep calling it forth, because not one of these details of prophecy that you call forth shall fail. None shall lack her mate in your life.

Declare thus:

I am a joyful mother/father of children!

I am a fruitful vine planted on a most fruitful hill!

I have received strength to conceive!

Children are my heritage from the Lord and the fruit of the womb is His reward!

I am fruitful and I multiply!

If you declare these and stand in faith, knowing fully well that God is not a man that He should lie and being fully persuaded that He spoke truth when He said He would bring children to pass, then your expectations shall not be cut off! None of these statements of faith shall fail nor lack her mate in fulfillment!

You will be challenged by what you see, of people's opinion, of monthly periods, of self-doubt, of old wives fables, of medical reports, of mood swings, of a history of childlessness running in the family, of expert opinions, of thoughts about your former life style, and/or of other experiences of life, but keep your fingers, your heart, and your mouth on the trigger of the word. Keep shooting out the word for your tongue "is the pen of a ready writer" (Ps. 45:1).

Your tongue is the pen, the ink is the word. Dip your tongue into the ink of the word and begin to speak. You are a ready writer. Write that your womb is now ready to carry your baby. Write that you are a joyful mother of children. Write that you are a fruitful vine planted in a most fruitful field. Write that you see yourself pregnant. Write that you are carrying your baby. Write that there shall be no complications during and after your delivery.

Write that you are a father of children. Write that you are full of good seeds that are able to impregnate your wife. Write that your wife is carrying your baby. Write that your children are proper and blessed children. Write, write, write.

John 1:14 reads, "And the word became flesh!" These words too shall become flesh in your womb and you shall soon carry your baby in your hands in Jesus precious name! The word of God will prevail! (Acts 19:20).

If you will keep at it, the word will prevail over every circumstance in your life. Keep calling forth the invisible, the word that is settled in heaven must settle in your life in Jesus' name! The twist and turns of life are no match for the settled word (Ps. 119:89).

You've got to believe that I am sent to you by God as His servant (Isa. 44:26). That is the only way God is going to confirm these words as I speak them to you. You've got to believe that I am His messenger to you in this season of your life. That is the only way He is going to perform His counsels through this book unto you.

Soon after our wedding, we agreed on the names of our children and their sequences and sex, so the name Shalom has always been part of our family. His name was not just mentioned on our family devotions, but we took time to mold his destiny through scriptural prayers though yet unborn.

My wife suggested that he should take to my height, and I agreed that he should take to her complexion. We carefully chose his physical features and agreed upon them and took time to put him on scriptural prayers for divine weaving.

We were so used to Shalom that one of my wife's e-mails was addressed as Shalom's mum. We never missed an opportunity to mention his name even before he was conceived. My wife designed computer graphics to that respect. You cannot look around our house without seeing the name Shalom starring at you.

My private and public prayers were well laced with the name Jehovah Shalom. Most people didn't know why I kept using that name, but my wife and I knew.

Several times, I would take to the dance floor with my wife in our sitting room to celebrate the arrival of Shalom.

Seeing us dance then, one may conclude that the baby was already on the couch, but most times, my wife had just seen her menses. It was a sacrifice of praise! Sincerely speaking, it wasn't easy on us, but we have learned that the best way to stop doubt is to give a shout of praise.

Were we ever depressed? Yes, depressions came knocking, but we locked our focus on the faith of God. That is the arena for the miraculous, not on being depressed. Nothing good ever happens when you are depressed. Are you aware that depression is not just your feelings, it's a demon spirit called the spirit of heaviness? (Isa. 61:3). Its primary assignment in your life is to make you mourn and sit in ashes of defeat and hopelessness but, if you will accept the beautifying oil of joy and the garment of praise, you will be as the tree of righteousness planted by the rivers of water that brings forth the fruits of your womb in your season (Ps. 1:3).

Did we ever cry? Oh yes, but the arms of our hands were made strong by the hands of the Almighty (Gen. 29:24).

The gravitational pull of doubt, fear, and unbelief could not pull us out of the magnetic field of scriptural faith. We stayed glued to the word of God and the declaration of our faith in Him. That made all the difference.

If you heard me preach on God's unfailing covenant of procreation, you would think I had a house full of children; you may never have had the faintest idea that we had none physically then. Well, that is how I understood faith should be practiced and preached.

Naturally, children were attracted to us. We loved our neighbors' children, so our home became a beehive of activity for children of all ages. Some would sleep off late into the night until their parents would come and carry them or we would carry them home ourselves.

When the children had all gone and we were left alone, the devil would exploit these contrasting fortunes. He attacked our minds and tried to tell us that God had been unfair and partial to us.

It was only a trap of deceit. We refused to give in to his mind games. We kept close to the word of God and our daily scriptural confession of faith, although it wasn't an easy thing to do. It took every last ounce of our faith in Him to keep at it.

Why are we going to this extent to explain all these things to you in details?

We want you to know that we are also a people subject to like passion as you are (Jm. 5:17) and have sat where you sit (Eze. 3:15).

We have faced what you are now facing. However, there is no temptation or challenge facing you but such as is common to man (1 Cor. 10:13).

God brought us through. He will bring you through with your miracle intact. We are here today standing as a living testimony, as will you in Jesus' name!

If the devil gets you to quit calling forth the invisible, you are finished. The devil is going to fight you dirty on this level more than in any other area because he is uncomfortable when you speak faith from your heart. He knows that at this point, his backbone is broken. It's just a matter of time for the manifestation of your breakthrough. His major weapon is discouragement. So be warned!

See those children through the eyes of faith. Rejoice for them. We called Shalom, Sharon and Praise until they came into being. Since it worked for us, it shall work for you as well in Jesus' name. God loves you so much. Start taking inspired steps of faith. I see you rejoicing. I can't wait to receive your testimony.

Let us pray:

Father, Dorothy and I agree and release our faith with this precious family for a quick manifestation of your goodness upon their home. We release our faith with theirs and agree that just as we have our babies, they shall carry theirs as well.

Lord! You broke through the barriers of negative reports to establish Your word of procreation in our family; Today, I decree and declare the establishment of your power of procreation in their home in Jesus' name! Thank you Father. In Jesus' name, amen

As you trust Him for this manifestation, the blood of Jesus has availed for you. The devil has lost out in your lives as touching this matter. Once again Lord, we celebrate Your faithfulness as we welcome this family into the world of parenthood.

3 WORD ALIGNMENT

So shall my word be that goeth out of my mouth; it shall not return unto me void, but it shall accomplish that which I please, and it shall prosper in the thing whereto I sent it (Isa 55:11)

This truth is extremely important. Your body aligns itself to the word of God that you declare. When your car is out of shape, you need to go for a wheel alignment. Jesus saw Simeon and called him Peter; Jesus saw a dead child and said she sleeps. Jesus told the ten lepers to go and show themselves to the high priest. They went in faith feeling nothing but, before they could get there, an alignment had taken place; their bodies were aligned to the word of healing He spoke and they were healed.

Jesus went to Lazarus' burial ceremony and exclaimed that He is the resurrection and the life, thus aborting the burial ceremony and turning their sorrows into and dancing.

He kept aligning the situations of life to the truth of the word of God because His word is the measuring rod of life. It doesn't matter what your body, situation, or someone else says. Until He speaks, no one has truly spoken. As it is written, "all things were made by Him and without Him was not anything made that has been made" (Jn. 1:3).

The same word can recreate and reposition your body system to carry out its God-ordained functions. Every nerve responds to His word. The entire process of reproduction is subject and obedient to the word. It's a double-edged sword. Nothing escapes its scrutiny; nothing escapes its miraculous touch. The word of God is the general overseer of the entire bodily system and has the final say on every conflict in the system (Heb. 4:12). In the same way, "Neither is there any creature that is not manifest in His sight; but all things are naked and open unto the eyes of Him with whom we have to do" (Heb. 4:13).

The Word rules the body with unparalleled grace and authority. It dethrones every negative situation in order to enforce the rule of heaven in our lives.

You know that whenever your car is not in shape, you take it to the mechanic for alignment. Whenever our body system is not in shape, we take it to God via scriptural declarations for system alignment. It's a duty we should not neglect or delegate to someone else. We must take responsibility for that.

You must consciously align your system with the word of God through scriptural confessions, not with empty words that have no effect but with faith in your heart. It is the process of engrafting the word (Jm. 1:21).

To engraft the word is to superpose the truth of the word of God over and above every negative report emanating from your body or any quarter. We do this by the twin forces of believing and confession of the word (Rom. 10:10).

We know fully well that Jesus is the high priest over what we profess. We are professors of His word (Heb. 3:1). He sits on high to enforce our proclamations of faith. Believing and saying the same things that God says about us in His word is the key to great victory. Not what we feel, not what you hear others say, and definitely not what the doctors have said but speaking out what God says in His word about us.

Period! For Christ confirms the words of His servants and performs the counsel of his messengers (Isa. 44:26).

If we refuse to confess His word, what will He superintend over?

That means that God is watching over your word-based confessions so as to bring them to pass. Irrespective of what the doctors have said, the word of God in your heart, spoken out of your mouth by faith and sustained with practical steps of faith, is bound to overthrow all other negative reports whether written or spoken. Christ "blot[s] out the handwriting of the ordinances that were against us, which was contrary to us and took it out of the way, nailing it to His cross" (Col. 2:14).

To engage the force of liberation which grace has already provided for you, you must learn to speak faith-filled words. You must learn the secret of word alignment. You must speak to your body and situation to line up with the word of God. You must daily insist by demanding that the word must reign in your life. You must order and decree that your sperm, your womb, and the entire reproductive system be aligned to what the word of God says concerning you.

Faith Speaks! (Rom 10:6)

Any faith that does not speak out the word of God is dead and unproductive. Until faith speaks out, nothing happens!

The word of God is like a match box. Until you pull out the match stick of the word of God and scratch it with bold speaking, you are not going to get any result.

To align means to bring into line, line up, arrange in line, make straight, make parallel, side with, support or ally. If our body is speaking another language apart from what God has said, we can bring it into line by the word of God that we speak in faith. When we take side with the word of God, irrespective of any other report around us, we are bound to experience a miracle after the trial of our faith.

Address your body by faith. Speak to your sperm to fall in line with the word of God. As you speak, believe that it shall be so and do not forget to look to the word instead of the circumstances that the devil will point out to you.

While playing volleyball as a freshman at the University of Lagos, someone forcefully hit the ball right on my eye. As time went on, I realized that a thick black cloud covered my eye and completely blocked my view. I couldn't see again through that very eye, not to speak of the excruciating pain that it brought. I laid my hands on it and declared that my eye be healed and have perfect vision restored. I was seriously tormented by thoughts of losing my sight, but I kept declaring that my eye was healed. I kept checking to see whether the eye had cleared until the Lord told me to believe and relax. I often caught my hand wandering to check the eye, and I would literally drag my hands down. Through a thankful heart, I took my mind off it completely and rested in God's faithfulness. After a very long time, one afternoon while I was in a lecture room, the Lord spoke to me and asked me to check my eye. Behold: it was completely restored! The devil tormented my mind with all kinds of thoughts about my eye, but I kept my mind on God's ability and faithfulness.

Command your womb to carry your baby in the name of Jesus. Speak with a very high level of conviction and authority. Speak as Jesus would, "for He taught them as one having authority, and not as the scribes" (Matt. 7:29).

To engraft means to superimpose or place something over the other. It means to place over, put on top, overlay, apply to or cover up. Engraft your reproductive system or any intimidating situation with the word of God and see your baby grow in your womb and the miracle delivered into your hands.

You will carry your desired baby in Jesus' name! You shall successfully and miraculously deliver your baby in Jesus' name. I believe in miracles! The word of God is the factory for miracles.

The responsibility to enforce this divine mandate is entirely yours. What grace has provided for, faith must collect! To accomplish this, you must learn to act in obedience to the word of God. By aligning yourself to the word of God that you speak by faith, you are already operating on the level of faith dimensional living.

....and it shall prosper in the thing whereto I send it (Isa. 55:11).

4 KNOWLEDGE VERSUS IGNORANCE

*My people are destroyed for lack of knowledge, because thou
hast rejected knowledge (Hos. 4:6)*

You will do well to give attention to this chapter. For a
long time, we exercised blind faith. We refused medical
diagnosis until we were advised by a senior colleague to go
for a medical test. He reasoned that if we go for a medical
test, we will be able to pinpoint the issues to tackle in
prayers.

If you refuse to gain appropriate knowledge about the
situation, how will you be able to channel your faith
properly? There is absolutely nothing wrong with getting a
medical diagnosis. In fact, your doctor should be a friend
and a partner in this process. All we are saying here is that
any medical report that forecloses your chances of carrying
your baby cannot be said to be correct from a scriptural
point of view. As we have been told, if anyone speaks "not
according to this word, it is because there is no truth in
them" (Isa. 8:20). No matter how sound any body of
knowledge is, until it complies with the scriptures, it is
deficient and, therefore, definitely not as sound as it ought

to be.

It was after I was handed two damaging medical reports from two separate medical laboratories that God spoke to me through Colossians 2:14, in which the scripture reads that it will blot out and overcome all ordinances against us. In fact, it has already through the nailing of Christ to the cross.

I compared these two reports with God's own report, and I chose to side with the report of God concerning me. He has the ability to blot out any other handwriting that is against His plans and purposes for my life.

Is there a report that is contrary to your expectation? God is a specialist at taking it out of your way, having already nailed it to His cross.

It takes faith to handle the issues of life. Your faith must be based on sound knowledge. You are not fazed by the facts of the matter medically, but you choose to believe the truth of the word of God. That is faith in action! According to 2 Corinthians 4:18, "While we do not look at the things which are seen, but at the things which are not seen; for the things which are seen are temporary, but the things, which are not seen, are eternal."

If you choose to focus on what God has said about you, what He has not said will soon fade away. It's only the word of God that is permanent, eternal, and unchangeable. All other reports are subject to change. There is nothing wrong with medical diagnoses or medication as long as they are in line with the word of God.

It is quite unfortunate that most cultures of the world view women as the culprit whenever childlessness rears up its head in a home, but we know that it is not always the truth. Both partners should go for a medical checkup so as to know how and where to channel their prayers.

Men should stop playing pretend on this matter. If you are living by faith, stay strong in it and patiently explain that to your spouse without being pretentious about it. This is a serious business and not child's play. Some men send their wives for a medical checkup while they stay back at home believing that it's their wives that have the problem. It is a manifestation of pride, hypocrisy, or simply fear that he might be indicted by a medical checkup. That's why some of our men folk steal away to see their doctors privately and warn them not to let their wives know the result of the test. But the Bible tells us that two can only walk together if they are of one accord (Amos 3:3), that two can put ten thousand to flight (Deut. 32:30), and that if two "shall agree on Earth as touching anything that you shall ask, it shall be done for them of my father which is in heaven" (Matt. 18:19).

With this in mind, what is all the secrecy about?

For the wife, nagging will only worsen the matter. A man by nature is a very proud being. It takes an understanding wife to make her husband do what ordinarily he would not like to do.

A good wife like you should know how to get your husband to do the right thing without injuring his pride as a man. No matter how stubborn they may appear, every man is a child at heart if you understand him. You need to have a united front in order to fight this common enemy and overcome it. The bible spoke of the perfect place of Eden as a land where man and wife were naked and not ashamed (Gen. 2:25). In the same way, you must be naked (open) to each other and not be ashamed. Secrecy exiles love and trust out of the home.

You cannot win this battle on a divided front. Where there is love, there is no fear. The true test of your love for each other is the degree of openness you have toward one another.

When our medical results came out, the doctors placed the blame on me. My wife was 'discharged and acquitted' by the medical results. I had to swallow my pride. With the help and comfort of my wife, I went to work, and the results are on the ground today.

You too can do it. But where suspicion has already taken root, I will suggest that you first confide in your pastor so that he will prayerfully know how to handle it.

In some cases, the medical diagnosis certifies the couple healthy, so why the delay? I will answer you: "an enemy has done this" (Matt. 13:28). This is where you need to arm yourselves with the sword of the spirit, which is the word of God, and with it uproot the gates of hell standing against your miracle in the form of delay.

Some people in this condition often go to sleep rejoicing that the doctors have given them a clean bill of health, yet days run into months and months into years. Lift up the battle cry, for it is time to contend for your babies. Yes, "rise ye up, take your journey…behold, I have given into thine hand [the battle]…begin to possess it, and contend with [the enemy] in battle" (Deut. 2:24).

'Rise ye up' is an action statement. Don't just sit down and think that by and by something will happen. Don't be fooled by that. This book is a road map on how you can contend and take your victory by the force of faith and prayers.

Declare times of fasting and prayer. Tell your pastor that you are sensing a foul play here. Contend for your victory. Follow the principles outlined in this book. Get in touch with a minister of the gospel that has grace along the line of breaking the yoke of barrenness. Let's not shy away from this truth out of pride; God has a specialist in every area of ministry.

Every root of delay in your family that touches your children is uprooted now in Jesus' name! The same God who remembered the wombs of Rachel, Leah, and Rebekah remembers you (Gen. 25 and 30). God remembers you! He has opened your womb and you shall conceive and deliver your children! Reproach shall be far from you in Jesus' name! When you pray together with your spouse as a family in love and faith, something great and wonderful happens. Whether you are unable to have children or you have a couple but wish for more, you will be blessed! It will happen! He has done it over and again.

You shall conceive again in Jesus' Name! I declare your womb open and ready to carry your baby in Jesus' Name! You cannot be denied.

I see you pregnant!

I see you delivering your babies!

I see you rejoicing as a fruitful mother of children!

I see your family jubilating!

Some couples may like to have twins but don't know the scriptures to anchor their faith on. Here are some that will definitely be of immense help to you. God is watching over His word to fulfill them if your faith and confessions are in line with His word.

- Song of Solomon 4:2: "Thy teeth are like a flock of sheep that are even shorn, which came up from the washing; *whereof every one bear twins and none is barren among them.*"

- Song of Solomon 6:6: "Thy teeth are as a flock of sheep which go up from the washing, *whereof every one beareth twins, and there is not one barren among them.*"

- Genesis 25:24: "And when her days to be delivered were fulfilled, behold, *there were twins in her womb.*"

- Genesis 38:27: "And it came to pass in the time of her travail that, behold, twins were in her womb."

Never forget: "with God, nothing shall be impossible!" (Lk. 1:37).

5 JACOB'S PROCREATIVE RECIPE

And Jacob took him rods of green poplar, and of the hazel and chestnut tree; and pilled white strakes in them; and made the white appear which was in the rods. And he set the rods which he had pilled before the flocks in the gutters in the watering troughs when the flocks came to drink, that they should conceive when they came to drink. And the flocks conceived before the rods, and brought forth cattle ringstraked, speckled, and sported …that they might conceive among the rods (Gen. 30:37-40)

When the revelation of the above scriptures dawned on my spirit man, I realized that God's purpose was and is still to terminate barrenness wherever and whenever it rears its ugly head in our lives. The principles of God are eternal and work for every generation.

Jacob's procreative recipe is a time-tested antidote for barrenness in all spheres of life, especially in terms of childbearing, and his instructions were quite clear. This is all about the force of meditation. Jesus is the rod which came forth *out of the stem of Jesse* who is also the word made flesh. (Isa. 11:1, Jn. 1: 1, 14). The rod is the word of God.

When we meditate on the word of procreation that we have discovered and gleaned from our diligent study of the word of God, we are simply pilling the white in them to reveal to God's deep-rooted desire to have us carry our babies. Whatever that we discover in the word through the force of meditation is bound to produce its material equivalent in life.

When you pill through the word and discover the keys to wealth, you shall possess wealth in life which grace has already made available. If you discover divine health after pilling through the word, it shall be yours. If you pill through and discover fruitfulness, barrenness cannot survive around you. Whatever you discover by pilling the word is yours to keep!

When our spirit man captures this living reality and embraces it with every fiber of our faith, there and then, this truth miraculously quickens our mortal bodies by

His Spirit which dwells in us (Rom. 8:11). Then, we can also conceive among the rod of the word of God. The birthing of this revelation in us gave us the supernatural boldness that we cannot be childless.

To pill, you need to sit down with the word of God in meditation. You need to saturate your spirit and mind with the truth of the word. It`s a process of incubation.

Action steps:

1. Search through the bible and discover what God has said about you on fruitfulness. For instance,
    a. Exodus 23:26: "There shall nothing cast their young, nor be barren in thy land."
    b. Song of Solomon 4:2: "Thy teeth are like a flock of sheep that are even shorn, which came up from the washing; *whereof every one bear twins and none is barren among them.*"
    c. Song of Solomon 6:6: "Thy teeth are as a flock of sheep which go up from the washing, *whereof every one beareth twins, and*

there is not one barren among them."

d.   Psalm 127:3: "Lo, children are a heritage of the Lord: and the fruit of the womb is His reward."

2.   Make Copies

Write or print them out and place them where you will always look at them, especially by the side of your mirror, refrigerator, car, diary, computer or handset screens, on the walls of your kitchen, bathroom, and wherever you spend much time alone. Don't forget to carry one in your handbag.

To help my faith, I cut pictures of newly born babies from a newspaper and wrote down scriptures on them that explained my expectation. Since my bible was my closest companion, I placed those pictures in there. Every day whenever I opened my bible, there they were staring at me. I wrote the names of my expected children on each of the babies' pictures. Long after they were born, I carried those pictures. Today, faith has become sight. Instead of carrying those pictures around, I carry my babies.

3.   Meditate

To Meditate is to think through, to excavate down to the root so as to reveal the truth behind the scene, locating yourself in the hidden truth in order to appropriate the blessings therein.

It is the pressing and squeezing aspect of the study of the word of God that causes the juice of its blessings flows into your life. This realm is unfamiliar to a casual reader of the word of God, yet this is where God's blessings are stored for you and me. Pilling through the word through the force of meditation reveals where the true power for breakthrough lies.

This is the point at which the word of God moves from letter to the hammer of the word that breaks the rock of childlessness into pieces. The Lord has said, "Is not my word like as a fire…and like a hammer that breaketh the rock in pieces?" (Jer. 23:29). When this truth was birthed in me, I knew that the truth has prevailed.

6 RIDICULOUS ACTS FOR THE MIRACULOUS

For the foolishness of God is wiser than men (I Cor. 1:25)
For as the heavens are higher than the earth, so are mine ways higher than your ways and mine thoughts than your thoughts (Isa. 55:8)

When God changed the names of Abram to Abraham and Sarai to Sarah and made them call themselves by those names among their neighbors, it sounded ridiculous, but it was the faith-fuse for their miracle. They must have been the object of ridicule among the folks who taught that they were going senile. How could two childless old people suddenly wake up this morning and start calling themselves "*Father of many nations and Mother of nations*" (Gen. 17:15-16) It was a ridiculous act that activated the miraculous.

God has said that we should avoid slothfulness but be "followers who, through faith and patience, inherit the promises" (Heb. 6:12).

When this truth dawned on us and since we realized that "God is no respecter of persons, we decided to take some practical steps of faith based on the word of God (Acts

10:35). We went and bought some baby items. After the purchase, I told my wife that we would carry these items back home on foot. Remember, our neighbors were well aware that we had no child.

On our way home, heads were turning. Our neighbors must have been wondering what was going on. We courageously carried our baby's nursing items home. It was a ridiculous act, but it activated the miraculous.

We came in and thanked God for the bold faith and the victory. We announced to heaven that our babies were alive, reminded the devil that children are God's heritage, and told ourselves that God cannot withhold any good thing from us, including our children. We even displayed the items at a very prominent place in our sitting room so that they were the first things any visitor saw on entering our house.

Some weeks later, one of our neighbors asked my wife who really owned the things we bought the other day. She asked my wife whether it belonged to one of her sisters. Thank God for faith for dominion. My wife told her that they were for *our* baby, of course. Heaven must have agreed with her, for few months after that, she took in for our first baby, Shalom.

Before this very incident, after saturating my spirit and mind with the word of procreation one Sunday morning, I announced to our church that my wife was pregnant and asked everyone to come close to the altar and join us in a dance of praise unto God for His faithfulness in fulfilling His word on us. We all rejoiced, danced, and praised God. I was operating from the scriptural point of view that says that "what *things so ever ye desire, when ye pray, believe that ye receive them, and ye shall have them*" (Mark 11:24).

Faith must have legs to walk on. I believe, therefore have I spoken. As for me, praise is the natural response to my believing. It's a ridiculous act that led us to the miraculous.

After this section of praise, our members became quantity surveyors, who watched daily to see how far my wife's belly was protruding. After they watched for more than nine months without any visible evidence, they must have been confused. You see, we have two varying viewpoints here. They were looking for a physical sign, while I had already seen the invisible.

In the process of time, that which I saw became visible to them. I refused to abort my faith because of what they could not see! When Shalom was born and they were jubilating and rejoicing, I knew that they were very late.

Faith must have legs on which it walks. Please give your faith its legs (Jm. 2:17, 22).

The root of faith is the word of God inspired in your heart, but your corresponding steps of faith based on the word of God is the greatest expression of your faith. Be led by the Spirit and learn to take faith steps.

My wife had a maternity gown that she wore almost all the time. It was a ridiculous act but it led to the miraculous. She wore it at home and to the market. When she wore that gown, there was no visible sign of pregnancy anywhere, but we walked by faith and not by sensory perception (2 Cor. 5:7). We forcefully took that which God has given to us by taking ridiculous steps that led us into the miraculous.

Taking steps of faith may look foolish, but therein is the wisdom of God. Who could have believed that a virgin could conceive and bear a child? Who could have believed that Sarah and Elizabeth would bear children at their old ages? When God is involved, just prepare yourself for the unthinkable! People must have laughed at us in mockery, but we laughed in faith, and today we are still laughing. The foolishness of God will always be wiser than men.

7 THE FORCE OF IMAGINATION

…and now nothing will be restrained from them which they have imagined to do (Gen. 11:6)

Until you have painted the picture of your parenthood, you are not likely to be a parent. Imagination is the act of image formation. Your mind is the canvas upon which you paint the pictures of your children even before they are conceived.

Conception takes place in your spirit before it takes place in your womb!

You must see it first before you feel it!

You must carry it on the inside before you carry it in your hands!

You must see yourself pregnant before you see yourself pregnant!

Every magnificent architectural edifice you see standing anywhere in this world first existed inside the mind of an architect!

I don't care what the doctors have said about your case, if you will lay hold of the instrument of imagination based on the word of God and repaint the negative pictures you are carrying about with positive ones, you will emerge carrying your babies. Great and outstanding results will follow you anytime you apply the principles of image formation.

When God wanted to bless Abraham with children, He gave him a picture of stars in the sky and sand by the seashore. Abraham kept brooding on those pictures, and it didn't take long before that which he had imagined became a reality.

Such strong creative imagination is the product of rigorous meditation on the truth of the word of God as per touching your expectation.

When God wanted to liberate Israel from the bondage of Egypt, He gave them the picture of a land flowing with milk and honey. God speaks in pictures.

If you study the word of God and strongly imagine yourself carrying your baby, no force in hell can stop that miracle. If you paint the picture of you as a joyful mother or father of children, God will always say, "Thou has well seen, for I will hasten my word to perform it" (Jer. 1:12). That which you see based on the word of God is the raw material God will use to perform and perfect your miracle. You must be on the same page with God.

Some of us need to overthrow the negative pictures that the devil has painted on our minds as to our ability to carry our own babies. The devil deals in lies. The infallible truth of the word of God is superior to the lies of the devil. The word has said that none shall be barren (Ex. 23:26).

So what do you say? You must perfectly picture yourself carrying your baby. You must buy into this truth beyond every reasonable and unreasonable doubt. You must enlist yourself among those that must carry their own babies. It's your unquestionable right in the kingdom and you cannot be denied.

When God said to be fruitful and multiply, He didn't say that can happen only if there are no defects in your reproductive system, nor did He say that only when medical science says so! God may choose to plant your baby anywhere as long as His word is established in your life and you carry your baby. No argument or medical condition is strong enough to nullify the word of God in your life if you choose to believe God and take Him at His word.

The next phase is to substantiate the picture in your imagination with a physical picture on the outside. As I said earlier on, even before we had our babies, I cut pictures of new babies and wrote the names of my children on them and carried them about for a very long time before they were born. Every time I looked at those pictures and read the scriptures, I wrote underneath them. I knew that we would carry those children and today, we have them.

Build a strong image of your baby in your mind based on the word of God. Give it a physical expression by placing a picture of your desired baby right where you can see it daily. What you see is very powerful. God's creative power is in your imagination. Put it into action.

8 TRACING THE FAMILY TREE

If the foundation be destroyed, what can the righteous do? (Ps. 11:3)

Oftentimes, there are perversions and distortions in the family lineage which we have come to accept as the status quo in our family life. Whenever you notice something unusual in the family history, such as strange patterns of occurrences or a common thread of circumstances that goes from generation to generation, you might do well to put the entire family under an intense scrutiny with the searchlight of the word of God.

In some families, it's like there is an unwritten code that some people, either the first born or the last born—whether male or female—do not get married. But, if by chance they do, they may never give birth or have delay in childbirth.

Whatever be the perversion, it's a lie of the devil. Trying to appease the devil in any way will only elongate his dominion over your family. The kingdom of heaven, "from the days of John the Baptist until now…[has suffered] violence, and the violent take it by force" (Matt. 11:12).

Don't you ever trivialize the matters of your family

history. It deserves close marking so as to bring every aspect of it to scriptural scrutiny. Don't just jump into prayers on this matter without knowing what you are praying about. If you don't know, ask the Holy Spirit to help you out. Be observant and ask questions from those who ought to know.

For some of us, our parents did desperate and despicable things either in their search for a baby or in their bid to ensure our protection, so to say. Little did they know that in their desperation, they were mortgaging the future happiness and peace of their children. The devil will always ask for his pound of flesh. Hence, people inherit curses they know next to nothing about.

How would you explain the situations whereby both couples have been certified medically healthy yet are without children after years of being married? Never you forget that the devil would like to hide under medical jargons and, of course, medical equipment is not designed to search him out. The enemy has always sought to destroy the harvest while we are sleeping (Matt. 13).

The tares of oppression in your family can be handled. The blood of Jesus is strong enough to set you and your entire generation free. Whatever be the distortion within your family that has arisen to prevent your childbirth is broken now in Jesus' name. The Holy Spirit shall cleanse and de-link you from every oppressive regime that seems peculiar to your family. People shall turn to acknowledge that your God, who has come to your help, is mighty indeed. Your broken-off and wild branches will be grafted back in (Rom. 11:17). Your belief will bring about great blessings from the Lord (Lk. 1:45).

Now is the right time to balance this equation. The truth must be told.

You have eternal life, so you are not bound by the vagaries of life (Jn. 3:16).

You are of the family of Jesus, not of Adam.

Your root is in Christ, not your biological lineage (Heb.

7:14-16).

In Adam, death reigned and all dies, but in Christ, you have the life-giving Spirit of God (Rom. 5:14; 1 Cor. 15:45).

In Adam, all have cancer, infertility, barrenness and other things, but in Christ, the law of the Spirit of life sets you free from all these things (Rom. 8:2; 1 Cor. 5:17).

You are born of God! You are infused with the very life of God almighty (1 Jn. 4:4, 6, 17).

You have the very DNA of God because you are His offspring (Acts 17:28-29). Eternal life, which you carry on your inside, permits neither barrenness nor childlessness of any kind!

This is the Truth that must be told!

Lessons to imbibe from the above scriptures:

a.   Family trees are very important.

b.   The family from which you are coming is said to be a wild olive branch.

c.   You have the privilege of being engrafted into a new family tree in Christ.

d.   Having been engrafted due to the blood of the covenant, you have been cut off from the negative influences of your biological family.

e.   You are now positioned to receive the promised blessing of procreation that is part of the covenant.

f.   You can now share God's rich nourishment that flows in this special olive tree into which you have been engrafted.

g.   The performance of these things that God has said is directly dependent on your ability to believe and act on the word of God.

Action steps:

1. Denounce the hidden works of unrighteousness

Now that you know that you have a new family tree,

there must be a deliberate effort on your part to de-link yourself from the oppression pervading in the family by renouncing all the hidden works of unrighteousness that have been holding you captive. The blood of Jesus will speak on your behalf as you stand on it as your instrument for liberation. It's not out of place to get a minister who operates along this line to agree with you in prayers.

2. Confess and act boldly on the truth that you have been engrafted into Christ's royal and fruitful lineage.

See yourself already fruitful and praise God for it. Let this truth dominate your waking thoughts. You are a branch of the righteous one. Jesus took your place, and you have been delivered from the kingdom of darkness into the marvelous kingdom of His dear son (Col. 1:13). No weapon fashioned against you shall succeed. In the kingdom of God, neither curses, nor childlessness, nor any other negative experiences can survive here.

You are a special breed. You are planted on a most fruitful hill as the planting of the Lord. Nothing here and no one here is barren. Children are your heritage here. This royal lineage is extremely secure. No childlessness survives here. Barrenness, miscarriages, sperm issues, fibroid issues, blocked fallopian tubes, or any such malady cannot hack into it. It's where the kingdom of God rules and no childlessness can survive there. Welcome to the wonderful world of parenthood!

9 PRACTICAL STEPS OF FAITH

*Yea, a man may say, thou hast faith, and I have works; show
me your faith without your works, and I will show you my faith
by my works...for as the body without the spirit is dead, so
faith without works is dead also (Jm. 2:18, 26)*

Shop for your baby's items

Faith, though a rest, is not passive but active. There is
rest in the finished works of Christ through grace, but there
is activity through the violence of faith in accessing what
grace has already provided for. Faith is always taking steps
to provoke divine intervention. The two components of
faith are belief and action. Until these two are in place, faith
will lack results.

In this kingdom, seeing is not believing. Rather,
believing is seeing. Your belief must translate to action
steps. It is not enough to believe God for your baby; go out
there and do the shopping for your baby. Give substance to
your faith.

We bought some baby clothes in anticipation of our
babies.

After a long time, we were tempted to give them out to

our neighbor's wife who had just given birth, but we cautioned ourselves on that because to us, those clothes served as the receipt for our baby. Moreover, the volume of prophetic declarations that had gone into those materials for our children was just too much to be given away. Finally, our baby boy was born, and you can as well gaze upon the first set of clothes that he wore.

Even when the nursing staff insisted that I must get another set of clothes because, according to them, newborn babies should not wear yellow clothes due to the fear of jaundice, I insisted on those clothes. Go for your baby's nursing items; you will see your baby wear them.

Choose your baby's sex

Every child is special and unique. They are and will always be a source of great delight to all parents. Scripture has shown us that some people were very specific in their requests to God regarding their babies. One of the things this does is boost your faith so that you can get from God whatever your heart desires.

Hannah was meticulous and direct in her request for a baby boy. She asked for the Lord to look upon her in her sorrow, to grant her a son, and that if He did, that he "will be [God's] for his entire lifetime and his hair shall never be cut" (1 Sam. 1:11).

When her baby was born, Hannah came to share her testimony, saying, "oh my lord, as thy soul liveth, my Lord, I am the woman that stood by thee here, praying unto the LORD. For this child I prayed and the Lord hath given me my petition which I asked of him" (1 Sam. 1:26, 37). Our God is no respecter of persons; He will grant your petition as well.

Dorothy and I asked for a male child first, and we got one. I needed to revise the trend in my family whereby all my brothers' firstborn were females and all my sisters' firstborn were male children. It was as though it was an unwritten code, and I decided to crack it, especially when my mind started playing tricks on me to brace up for the status-quo. Others have asked for females, and they got theirs. If your baby's sex doesn't matter to you, go ahead and get ready for your miracle baby. Babies are special whether male or female. Yours is next in the line. Go for it now.

Choose your babies' names

Names are extremely important, for it often defines the destiny of the bearer. Nabal's foolishness was a synonym for his name (1 Sam. 25:25).

Jabez's misfortunes in life were traceable to his name (1 Chron. 4: 9-10). God had to change the names of Abram and Sarai before they could enjoy the blessings of covenant procreation that resulted in Isaac's birth (Gen. 17), while the unstable behavior of Peter was a reflection of his former name Simeon, Jesus called out the rock that was in him. Names are very important.

The habit whereby ungodly grandparents are given the exclusive right to determine the names of ybabies in certain cultures is a rumbling volcano that will soon explode. You must be in firm control of the names your babies bear. You have a duty to protect their fragile destiny through strong parental cover.

God takes great delight in giving the names of great and prominent people before they were born. John and Jesus are our foremost examples. Names often encapsulate a child's destiny. Don't wait until you see the pregnancy; prayerfully choose the name of your baby as an act of faith. Always pray for the baby with that name. Prophesy over and bless your child through that name. Shalom, Sharon and Praise were household names in my family before we even cradled them in our bosoms.

Very soon, people will get to know the name of your baby, and they will start addressing you as such. The majority will call out of faith while a few, as usual, will use it for mockery. We have all been victims of the latter, but concentrate on the positive angle to it. When they call you by the name of your baby, it creates a picture of parenthood that will become the major instrument in the hand of God to bring to pass what He has said.

That was the miracle-picture that Abraham and Sarah captured after the change of their names that led to the birth of Isaac. Picturing yourself as a parent is a very powerful weapon in the process of procreation. Until you see yourself there, you may never get there. Answering the names of your baby when called by it will go a long way in erasing the negative mental strongholds that the devil has built into your mind. To those in the western world, it may
sound strange, but in other cultures, it's not unusual to call a mother Shalom Mum.

When people call you by the name of your expected child, don't feel shy or surprised. Respond with enthusiasm, for that is one of the ways to call forth those things that be not as though they were. It is an exercise of your faith. It shall be rewarded. They called my wife Shalom Mum. Today she is Shalom Mum as Shalom is now here.

It's your turn. Go for it.

Tithe for your baby

It takes the mysteries of God to destroy the miseries of life.

In Hebrews 7, God says that Levi, the great grandson of Abraham, was inside him when he paid tithe to Melchisedec. Therefore, by extension, Levi, who was yet unborn, had paid tithe to Melchisedec, whom he never met.

The seed from which your baby shall come is already in you. Therefore, exercise your faith in that direction and open a tithe record for your desired baby as a sign of your faith. It's not the sum that matters but your faith coming alive to grasp your miracle.

Each time you raise up that tithe card for prayer as a symbol of your complete faith in the infallible word of God and call the name of your baby, you are only fast-forwarding your miracle.

God respects and honors faith; He will respect and honor yours today.

Sow seed for your baby

The law of sowing and reaping works in every area of life (Ecc. 10:19). Please note that the entire wealth of the world combined is not even enough to create any part of a baby's anatomy. The emphasis here is to project your faith through the law of sowing and reaping.

Recently, I was invited to a church to minister, after which I called for a seed since it was their pastor's appreciation day. Unknown to me, a couple who had suffered a lot of miscarriages after their first baby was born years before keyed into it for another baby. The wife later took in and delivered a baby girl. Their seed only served as a booster to their faith and, by faith, they took what the grace of God has already provided for them.

To further strengthen your faith, it's not out of place for you to sow a handsome seed toward the birth of your baby. Since money answers all things, when you release your faith through seed sowing into your expectation as touching your baby, it is bound to answer.

Don't just sow anywhere, sow into ministers or ministries where the anointing for procreative power is flowing very strong and visibly.

Rejoice and be grateful

Rejoice and be grateful "for the Lord is a God of knowledge and by Him, actions are weighed" (1 Sam. 2:3).

Your countenance is a powerful mirror that reflects what is on the inside. The face cannot successfully hide the joy that is in the heart. When we rejoice, we testify that God is good. When we rejoice, we demonstrate our complete trust on the integrity of the word of God as touching our lives.

When Hannah received the word, the bible says that she was sad no longer, as the Lord had remembered her (1 Sam.

1).

The Lord remembered her when the clouds of sorrow, self-pity, faultfinding, bitterness, jealousy and acrimony that were covering her gave way to the brightness of joy and faith.

You can't be carrying the whole world on your inside and expect to carry a baby there as well. You are already preoccupied. That would be too much weight for you. Please drop the weight of worry so as to carry your baby. One must leave for the other and the choice is all yours. If you want God to step in, then release yourself from your self-inflicted burden. Trust in the Lord will lead to perfect peace (Isa. 26:3-4).

Until you bring your mind to rest in God's faithfulness, there is really nothing anybody can do for you. The strength you need for conception and delivery can only be accessed through faith in God alone. As in Ruth, you must learn how to sit still and confidently rest in God's faithfulness, knowing fully well that He is in charge here (Ruth 3:18).

You must stand up from the throne of your heart, stop the pointing of fingers both toward yourself and others, and allow the Holy Spirit to be enthroned on your inside. The joy He gives is enough to activate your miracle. The Lord is a God of knowledge, and by Him your actions of faith will testify for you.

Again, learn to joyfully celebrate with others as they rejoice over the arrival of their babies, for what you celebrate is bound to get to you.

10 DEMYSTIFYING THE MYTH OF AGE

Then Abraham fell upon his face and laughed and then said in his heart, shall a child be born unto him that is a hundred years old? And shall Sarah that is ninety years old bear? (Gen. 17:17)

Now Abraham and Sarah were old and well stricken in age; and it ceased to be with Sarah after the manner of women (Gen. 18:11)

One of the major issues that leads people into stressful living is the question of age. For women, it is menopause and for men, it's the lack of ability to carry on their conjugal functions. But God, and not our physical anatomy, is the seed of procreation. God's word is behind fruitfulness, and it is neither restricted by circumstances nor by our chronological age.

While at the ripe age of ninety-nine and Sarah at ninety, God told Abraham to expect a son. His natural response to such a supernatural declaration was to laugh. He weighed God's word on the scale of their biological anatomies and concluded that it was impossible.

The devil's game plan when other schemes fail is to play a mind game on our age.

We can't intimidate the ancient of days with our age. He is the ageless one. A thousand years is like a day in His sight, so in His sight you are still a baby, your age notwithstanding. You must be careful not to limit the unlimited God (Ps. 78:41).

God's word is superior to your age. Menopause is not a threat to God. It is called *meno-pause* and not *meno-stop*. When you pause a thing, you can restart it all over again at your will and pleasure. God can and will restart it again or give you your baby with or without it. No biological argument, plausible or implausible, is strong enough to overthrow the veracity of the word of God as touching your fruitfulness.

Whatever the devil, hiding under medical sciences or spiritual wickedness, says about you that does not line up with the word of God is a lie. The measuring rod for your life is the rod of the word of God. You are productive. Your age is a certificate for a powerful testimony. Be encouraged by the words of the Psalms, which claim that "those that be planted in the house of the Lord shall flourish in the courts of our God... They shall still bring forth fruit in old age; they shall be fat and flourishing" (92:13-14).

In as much as it is medically wise to give birth at the bloom of your life, it is also imperative to note that delay is not denial. Your faith in God can put your baby into your arms. Even if you are above ninety years old, Sarah's record was set to be broken. We can then ask God to set a new record with you but until then, note that God's been there, done that, and seen it all. So, fall in line for your miracle now.

11 DIFFUSING STRESS

Casting all your care upon him, for he cares for you (1 Pt. 5:7)
Be careful for nothing, but in everything by prayer and
supplication with thanksgiving, let your request be made known
unto God (Phil. 4:6)

It has been said that about ninety percent of things in our lives are right and only ten percent are wrong. Stress is simply the overheating of our system, whether knowingly or unknowingly, which results in physical or mental complications that may cost one dearly.

Suffice it to say that it is mainly wishful thinking for one to live under stress and expect to take in. Our bodies need some form of equilibrium before they can conveniently discharge its duties. If our minds are constantly in turmoil, our body systems are bound to malfunction. For God to create Eve, He needed to put Adam into a position of perfect rest (Gen. 2:21).

When it comes to conception and delivery, worry is an exercise in futility. It is anti-faith and so anti-scripture. When we chose not to worry about the negative medical reports I had about myself, we experienced peace, as we knew that God's word would always work no matter the challenging situation we were facing.

It's not possible for you to have a firm faith in God and still be under stress. We were victims of stress ourselves, especially during my wife's monthly period. At times, the devil would play his mind games on me by predicting the exact day my wife would see her menses and, more often than not, it would be so.

It was a very tough time for us. We were looking at the wrong direction. But when the truth about diffusing stress came to us, whenever the blood appeared again, we would sing and dance before God and thank Him that our babies are our heritage is from the Lord, which nothing can stop. It was not just a formality but also an excited moment of deliberate praise to Him whose word cannot fail in our lives. By the time we got to this level, we knew that we had broken the backbone of childlessness.

We are not unmindful of the level of stress that most women in diverse cultures of the world are going through, as it is customary to blame them whenever there is a delay in procreation in the family. This, of course, is very simply unfair. All we are asking you to do is to follow our example and obey the scriptures. Cease from stress and build up your faith in the word of God. Your confidence in God is a mighty weapon for victory. It may not happen in a day but keep working at it until you know that you know that God cannot fail.

Hannah was a great example of this truth. After the man of God Eli had spoken into her life about her desire to have a baby boy, the bible recorded that lost her countenance of grief (1 Sam. 1:18). Later, she testified her faith, saying, "the Lord is a God of knowledge, and by him actions are weighed" (1 Sam. 2:3).

She came stressed up. She received the word and prayer. Then she went her way, ate, and was sad no more. You must operate in the faith of Jesus, which is already yours and walk away with your miracle (Gal. 2:20). She collected her baby and went home. The evidence of her faith was her joyful countenance.

It's now your turn. You shall carry your baby. Your actions are the voice of your faith, may it speak well of you before God. You are already approved in the beloved (Eph. 1:6).

Some of the reasons why childlessness persist among couples lies in their mutual suspicion of one another, especially when medical sciences or spiritual wickedness points an accusing finger at one of the partners as being responsible for their childlessness. That is an infantile trick of the devil.

Instead of the couple coming together to form a strong shield for each other, acrimony, bitterness and hatred are allowed to brew and fester in the home. Unfaithfulness and accusations become the order of the day. The devil will take a special delight in taking full advantage of the situation to create animosity. The couple becomes strange bedfellows, sometimes choosing to sleep in different bedrooms as well as keeping late nights so as to avoid the seething pot of trouble at home.

When you are divided, your strength is divided, and there is nothing you can do under such a circumstance to obtain your miracle. All you have to do is to retrace your footsteps back home. Apologize for those hurtful words, actions, and inactions. Genuinely seek for peace. It may not be so easy, but with love and tenacity, it can be done. Go the extra mile. Ask God for help. Swallow your pride and fight for your God given home.

God praises wise women who build up their homes but admonishes the foolish who put it down (Prov. 14:1). Alternatively, He instructs men to recognize the blessing of his wife and not deal treacherously with her (Mal. 2:14-15).

Stop every form of wickedness against each other because God has already planted some godly seeds in your bosom. Whatever you are doing to each other that raises the temperature at home to a boiling point must be repented of and stopped forthwith. Pretending that it's only your partner that is at fault is an evil wind that blows no one any good. The strategy of the devil is to break your rank. For God to do any work in your family, you must seek peace, love, forgiveness, mercy, and understanding in that home.

Keep your emotions in check with one another and in your spirit so that "your prayers be not hindered" (1 Pt. 3:7). Your prayers can be hindered if you allow the devil to manipulate your emotions. Sometimes, the devil will stir up a problem around the period of the woman's ovulation, and the couple will busy themselves with acrimony, hatred, and bitterness until it is all over. Then, they will reconcile only to start the same process all over again the next month. Don't let the devil take you for a ride again.

Also, in a home where sex is used as a weapon by either member of the couple to get even against God's express command, you can't expect God to work. The best you get is tension caused by bitterness and a sense of betrayal (1 Cor. 7:5). It's quite funny how you deny your partner sex with the flimsiest of excuses and yet desire to carry your baby. Sex is not a reward for good behavior; it's a right that must be frequently enjoyed by both members of a couple. When sex becomes a weapon wielded by either or both partners, God's cover cannot be said to be in that home.

Again, the idea of giving your child total affection while abandoning your spouse to himself is an open invitation to family crises. You child, no matter how much you love him, is not your spouse. Maintain the balance always.

Stress in the family is an evil wind that blows no one any good. Please take steps today to diffuse it. Don't let pride ruin your family's joy. Talk to God about it and He will help you to do the right thing. Be bold and apologize to one another and pray for each other that you may be healed. God gave you that home, fight the fight of faith for it. Forgive and get re-united. I see you overcoming.

12 THE TRUTH ABOUT MISCARRIAGES

There shall nothing cast their young nor be barren in thy land; the number of thy days I will fulfill (Ex. 23:26)

… and underneath are the everlasting arms… (Deut. 33:27)

He maketh the barren woman to keep house, and to be a joyful mother of children. Praise ye the Lord (Ps. 113:9)

When God said that nothing should cast their young nor be barren among his people, He wasn't making a suggestion. It was an absolute statement! The power behind His throne is behind that declaration, and He is not ready to compromise it for anything. But what you do with what God has said is up to you.

You see, God is not addressing all the women here but His covenant daughters, so it's very erroneous for you to generalize that all women are prone to miscarriage. It's not true at all. There is a set of people whose destinies are unique and enviable. They are called the daughters of Zion. They are not permitted to suffer what other women are prone to suffer except they are ignorant of the covenant provisions for their immunity from such vagaries of life.

It's not just your womb alone that is carrying your baby, there is an everlasting arm that is underneath whose responsibility it is to carry both you and your baby, and it has never miscarried anything entrusted into its care. The Lord is a refuge whose hands no man can pluck His people from (Deut. 33:27; John 10:28-29). He will keep His people safe (2 Tim. 1:12).

It's absolutely impossible for anything induced by the devil to pluck your baby out of the everlasting arms of God. It's impossible! Until you agree that your baby is gone, it's still there. No matter how long you see blood flow, the devil cannot snatch away your baby from the eternal arms of God.

Sister Ndidi was barely a month pregnant when she went in for surgery. She and her husband had asked God for a set of twins, though neither of them had a history of twins in their lineage. After the surgery, she bled every single day for the next three months. On the fourth month, they went for a scan, and the doctor was stupefied to discover that a set of healthy twins were still growing in her womb.

When you see the blood, what do you say? That is where the fight of faith begins. First and foremost, you can't miscarry. When the doctor coldly informs you that you have miscarried, how do you respond? You may not need to convince the doctor since he might not be on the same faith frequency with you, making it pointless trying to convince him otherwise. Your statement of faith is enough. His conclusion is based on his medical experiences; yours must be based on the wavelength of your experiences with God and His word.

Someone sent me this testimony from Germany:

I will also share my testimony with you. Help me celebrate our God, together with your church. My wife was supposed to give birth again on the 11th of this month here in Germany. But, on the 31st of March, I had to rush her to the emergency room of the best hospital in Germany. She was discharged after four hours because of her womb. Two days later, at 5am, my wife woke up intending to go to toilet, only to find herself in a heavy pool of blood. Her mattress had soaked the flowing blood under our bed without us knowing what was going on. As she stood-up, blood gushed out like it was water. I thought it was over for my child, but I had to save my wife's life. I called the emergency line and within minutes, they picked her up. The doctors said there was no rational reason for my child to survive because the placenta had discharged on her long ago, resulting in too much blood loss. However, both my wife and my baby survived without a problem, though they remained in intensive care for 12 days. The chief doctor gave me back her cross necklace, saying, "Keep your faith—Jesus is alive!"

-Tai Akin

You have a responsibility to uphold the banner of truth that has been committed to your trust in spite of the oppositions of medical science. Whenever medical science opposes your faith and leaves you hopeless, take your position in the word of God and refuse to yield ground to doubt and fear (1 Tim. 6:20-21; 1 Pet. 1:7). Your faith is only on trial!

Testimonies abound of women who, despite bleeding for days and months, insisted that their babies were intact, and God supernaturally sustained their pregnancies. You see, it's a war of words. Faith-fill your words! Use no empty words which are not rooted in the word of God.

God says that none will miscarry (Ex. 23:16)! However, we sometimes feel the devil say to us that when we see blood, we have miscarried. Whichever of these two you agree with, your every fiber has weight enough to swing you into victory or defeat. It is easy to know through your utterances, facial expressions, and body movements where you stand. If you believe what the ungodly and natural women believe, you will suffer what they suffer. Their rock is not your Rock. Theirs is standing on sinking sand. Yours is the Rock of ages that never fails; even the doubters know this.

Did you believe God for a flow of blood or for a healthy baby? Have you ever seen the anatomy of a baby such as its leg, hands, and head or even its tiny torso in the blood so discharged? If none, then how did you ever come to the conclusion that the mere passage of excess blood equates the loss of your baby? Someone must be hiding in the darkness of ignorance and pulling a fast one on women. Until your faith fails, your baby is intact. Stop falling for the intrigues of the devil for underneath, your baby is the everlasting arm that cannot miscarry.

At this stage, don't just keep quiet at the mind games of the devil. You have a declaration to make! Declare that your baby is not mere blood. Insist by the word of faith that your pregnancy is intact and anchored on the infallible word of God. Neither tears nor feeling sorry for yourself can solve this. It's faith that routs out the devil. Romans tells us that only God is true and all others are liars (Rom. 3:4).

Take time to give God quality praise for supernaturally sustaining your pregnancy. Don't ever give in to fear, for it is the major weapon of the enemy. Fear is a trap! Resist it. Arm yourself with the word of faith and with praise. Nothing the Lord defeats can rise up a second time (Nah. 1:9).

God cannot supernaturally sustain Jesus in the womb and yet abandon your own baby to the wiles of the devil. That is inconsistent with His nature. We are of the same family. Since our elder brother was shielded by the Holy Ghost while in the womb, rest assured that your baby is in good hands and no amount of devilish tricks can snatch your baby away from God's everlasting arms. Take your stand for your baby and the devil will go into hiding.

When my wife was a few months pregnant with our first baby, a bus knocked her down at a bus stop. She landed flat on her womb. She asked that the driver be allowed to go. She boarded another vehicle and went to work. It was never a prayer point. We knew that a miscarriage was not part of the covenant that God had with Jesus on our behalf. It was not an issue to be discussed. It just can't happen. The covenant of God is stronger than any force in life.

Stop buying into the old wives' fable that whenever you

take in, you must experience early morning fever, dizziness, and other disturbing symptoms. It's not written anywhere in the bible. Rather, strength and vigorous vitality are written about the women of God (Ex. 1:19).

The synonyms for the word vigorous are dynamic, vital, forceful, strong, hearty, enthusiastic, and spirited. This is God's program for your health throughout the season of your pregnancy and after. You must walk into it.

Isaiah tell us that unless the law and testimony speak according to the word of God, there is no light in them (Isa. 8:20). If it's not in the book, it has no ground to stand in your life! You are a living stone (1 Pet. 2:5)! You have everlasting strength (Isa. 26:3)! Enjoy your seasons of pregnancy and bounce around as a cricket.

Put your hand on your womb as I pray with you:

In the name of Jesus, I break that vicious cycle of miscarriages. I speak to this body: Line up with the word of God in Jesus' Name! You are not permitted to cast your young any more. Every conspiracy of hell to torment this body with miscarriages is overthrown now in Jesus' name.

I speak peace into this body! I decree the entire reproductive system free from every scourge in Jesus' name. The power of the Holy Ghost is brooding upon you. I see your womb ready for procreation. You shall carry your babies till the duration of the pregnancy in Jesus' name. You shall deliver in peace. The storm is over! Calm has returned. It's your turn now to laugh. You are free in Jesus' Name!!!

13 THE BLOOD CONNECTION

The cup of blessing which we bless, is it not the communion of the blood of Christ? The bread which we break, is it not the communion of the body of Christ? (1 Cor. 10:16)

The blood of Jesus is the final statement of God on every conflict of life. It takes the mysteries of the blood to destroy the miseries of life. It's unfortunate that we have yet to grasp the immensurable riches and power hidden in the blood of Jesus. No matter how mad the devil is, he cannot cross the bloodline. The hard situations of life crumble at the doorstep of the blood. The spirit of death was sensible enough to keep away from houses marked with blood in Egypt without asking whether it was a Hebrew or Egyptian that was inside (Ex. 12:13).

Nothing silences the voice of the devil as much as the mystery of the communion table whenever and wherever it is administered and received in faith. The communion table is more than the ritualistic symbol that we practice today (Matt. 26:26). It is a revelation of the limitless possibilities in the body and blood of Jesus. It is God getting personally involved in our lives by the power of His blood sacrifice. It is God placing his integrity, faithfulness, authority, holiness, mercy and righteousness on the line for us. No situation has ever stood in defiance of the blood. Nothing is so deaf that it cannot hear the *'Ephphatha'* voice of the blood. It opens every door, including the door of the womb for conception and supernatural childbirth. The voice of the blood that shook the earth can uproot the very foundations of childlessness in your life and generation.

It's not possible for you to be childless or miscarry again! In the first place, it's not you carrying your baby, underneath is the everlasting arm of our God who has never miscarried anything. Please, let that sink deep into your spirit man.

Communion is not just the symbol of the body and blood of Jesus Christ. It *is* the body and blood of Jesus Christ. When you partake thereof, you become one with Him. Whatever that is not permitted in His life must not be traced to you. Can you imagine Jesus miscarrying? It just can't happen! Can you imagine Jesus experiencing difficulties in getting pregnant? It can't happen! As He is, so are you (1 Jn. 4:17). Never forget that we are joined with Him in one spirit (1 Cor. 6:17).

You cannot be one with Jesus and also suffer the plague of miscarriage. Jesus never suffered miscarriages; He successfully delivered the church on the resurrection morning. So, no manner or pattern of miscarriage is allowed in the kingdom. Ignorance has made a victim of you, but revelation has now made a winner out of you.

The prophet Ezekiel wrote, "when I passed by thee, and saw thee polluted in thine own blood, I said unto thee when thou wast in thy blood, live; yea, I said unto thee when thou wast in thy blood, live" (Eze. 16:6). That you have seen blood is not the final conclusion that your baby is gone. God has equally seen you in that condition and has decreed that both you and your baby shall live. The author of life himself has decreed it. The owner of life and the giver of breath has spoken. Whose report will you totally believe, your doctor's, your feelings' or the eternal God's?

When you partake of the communion in faith, fibroid will disappear, medical conditions will be corrected, sperm counts will be rectified, fallopian tubes will be unblocked, conceptions will take place, the scourge of miscarriages will be defeated, and childlessness will be terminated.

When God cut a covenant with His people, He cut away barrenness and miscarriages from them. The good news is that we walk under a better covenant, ratified not with the blood of bulls or goats but the perfect blood of Jesus, the Lamb of God slain from the foundation of the earth. Your case is settled right now. Barrenness is not just a biological state, it is a spiritual force that manifest itself in biological disorders because in the beginning it was not so.

In as much as you are encouraged to receive all the medical help that you can afford, yet do not ever forget that you don't fight spiritual battles with only medical gloves. When your victory is settled in the spiritual, the biological manifestation will be a forgone conclusion.

I was told that most of my sperm were dead, and the living ones were said to be weak, watery, and bizarre, not to speak of staphylococcus and other medical jargons with which they described my supposed case. That was the medical report. Then I took my bible to cross-check on God's own report. It told me that I am complete in Him (Col. 2:10), that God has blotted out the ordinances against me (Col. 2:14), and that He will not withhold good from me (Prov. 3:27).

Based on these truths, I decided to consciously line up myself with this revelation. I decided to discard the report of the doctors and medical laboratories. One report must be superior to the other. The medical reports said that I was incomplete. God's report says that in Christ I am complete. A compendium of books and rigorous medical analysis ratified the medical reports while the blood of Jesus ratified God's report, so I chose to believe God's report.

God's report declared that He not only removed medical deficiencies but also nailed them to His cross. Whatever the doctors had seen, He took out of the way for me. Whatever were the conclusions of medical laboratories and spiritual wickedness, He has nailed them on the cross. I just praised and thanked Him for nailing all those things there and triumphing over them in it by His shed blood. I am a beneficiary of His accomplishments. He is not *going* to do that, He has already done that. I am a receiver. It was a fight of faith.

I confessed that God who said he will withhold not good will not break His word by withholding children from us when it is in the power of His hands to provide children and, neither will He delay them when He has the power to perform His word, especially now that the blood of Jesus is speaking in my favor. He cannot withhold what He has already given!

Today, the yoke is broken and we have three wonderful children, Shalom, Sharon, and Praise to show that God is committed to glorifying Himself by honoring our simple faith in Him. The speaking blood of Jesus could not be silenced by the murmurings of childlessness in our lives. It will always speak forth fruitfulness into our lives.

There is power in your prophecy. Say what God has said with faith and experience God's touch. It's your turn to rejoice. Impotency is no threat to God. The power that raised Jesus from the dead is still raising people and things from dead situations. It's still raising dead wombs and dead sperm. It's still healing uteri, ovaries, and fallopian tubes. It's still healing body heat and impotency. It's still doing what no man can do in your life! Line up your faith to the word of resurrection and experience the resurrection power in your reproductive system. His blood has availed for you. Nothing escapes the powerful searchlight of the Holy Spirit. He will restore, renew, resurrect, and heal you.

I know He is already brooding on you to bring forth your miracle. The speaking blood of Jesus is speaking your miracle.

14 THE ANOINTING

And it shall come to past in that day, that his burden shall be taken away from off thy shoulder, and his yoke from off thy neck and the yoke shall be destroyed because of the anointing (Isa. 10:27)

There is something special about the presence of God. When the presence of God invaded the valley of dry bones by the spoken word through Ezekiel, resurrection and life took over. Nothing negative, including childlessness survives in His presence for it is written that "everything that liveth, which moveth, whithersoever the rivers shall come, shall live: and there shall be a very great multitude of fish, because these waters shall come thither: for they shall be healed; and everything shall live whither the river cometh" (Eze. 47:9).

The anointing is like the torrent of a flowing river; nothing in its path escapes its touch. You can't stay in the presence of God and remain untouched if you come with your heart focused on Him. When a blind man named Bartimeus and the woman with the issue of blood stood in the path of Jesus, the flood of His presence did not spare their infirmities. When the nine lepers and the man that sat by the sheep market at the pool of Bethesda for thirty eight years came in contact with Him, they lost their ailments and went home to their families and friends completely healed. He called off several burial ceremonies when His presence invaded the place.

What is childlessness? Anyone who believes in God can experience the power of resurrection that freely flows from Him.

Standing on this apostolic auction, I decree and I declare that every burden of childlessness, barrenness, miscarriages, low sperm or no sperm count, medical complications, and every yoke of delay traceable to your life and any other yoke harassing your life and threatening your joy in life and family, by the reason of His anointing, is broken now in Jesus' Name! You are set free and delivered in Jesus' Name!

15 WALKING IN WISDOM

Have respect unto the covenant for the dark places of the earth are full of the habitations of cruelty (Ps. 74:20)

Wisdom is profitable to direct. The spiritual environment under which some of us come from calls for utmost caution in handling the issues of pregnancy. Until your testimony is perfect, there is no need to show off anything. As you give yourself over to praise, prayer, and confessions of the word of God after your conception, please remember that it's not time for you to announce to every Tom, Dick, and Harry that you have taken in. In fact, be as economical with the announcement as you possibly can, especially during the first five months of your pregnancy. Apart from your husband, pastor, and doctor or your godly parents, every other person can wait to see your womb gracefully changing shape.

When Elizabeth took in, she hid herself for five months to avoid the reproach of man (Lk. 1:24-25). The covenant of fruitfulness shall be established in your life, but you need to apply wisdom in its preservation.

To be pregnant is not enough but to carry your baby.

Don't go showing off your pregnancy but rather wait to testify of your baby as a living testimony of what God can do. When Sarah learned from God that she give birth, she said that the Lord made her laugh and would make others laugh at the seeming impossibility of her pregnancy (Gen. 21:6-7). Sarah didn't celebrate her pregnancy; she celebrated the birth of her baby. Do you get that? Don't start calling everyone to announce your pregnancy. Let them hear that you have delivered your baby. If you have an announcement to make before delivery, go to chapter twenty of this book. You have more than enough declarations there; choose the ones appropriate for you. It's better for people to gather and celebrate with you after your delivery. Don't put the cart before the horse. Stay on your ground of faith until your testimony is perfected and you carry your baby.

Sarah didn't carry her pregnancy to all the places where they ridiculed her to show it off. She didn't go back to all the places where she had lived childless with Abraham to shut their big mouths. It wasn't necessary. But, when the right time came, those people heard and saw that Isaac had been born. Your baby needs protection; don't over expose the child before the right time.

God returned to fulfill his word in the life of Sarah. He shall fulfill it in your life as well in Jesus' name! God is not partial in His dealings. You shall receive your bundle of laughter. Be wise!

16 DELIVERANCE FROM THE TRAP OF FEAR

For as much then as the children are partakers of flesh and blood, he also himself likewise took part of the same; that through death he might destroy him that had the power of death, that is the devil; And deliver them who through fear of death were all their lifetime subject to bondage (Heb. 2:14-15)

In the course of my ministrations, I have met women who were simply afraid of death during childbirth. I also have come to understand that such fears are simply based on ignorance. All they need is an understanding of the covenant provisions available to them. I strongly suggest that you open the scriptures and learn to handle the spirit of fear. I want to help you by the Holy Spirit overcome this once and for all.

Some have seen or heard of women dying during childbirth. Some are in bondage to old wives' fables. Others are afraid due to their medical histories. Those tormenting thoughts of death are satanic attacks on your mind. Jesus died that you might live. Does that make sense to you? You have been delivered from death; don't be in bondage to the fear of death. Without the fear of death, the devil is powerless in your life. When you entertain the fear of death, you are deliberately empowering the spirit of death.

When Job was experiencing his temptation, he shared in this human feeling. "For the thing, which I greatly fear, is upon me, and that which I was afraid of is come unto me. I was not in safety, neither had I rest, neither was I quiet, yet trouble came" (Job 3:25-26). What Job feared for most, he received. Job activated the disasters that came into his life and family through fear. He brooded upon them for years, thereby giving Satan the legal ground to attack. Job was neither in safety, rest, nor quietness, irrespective of the divine defenses around him, so trouble come to him.

The fear of death is a bondage to the spirit of death. You shall not die but live to declare the glory of the Lord in the land of living. You have been redeemed from death. Satan will never attack you until he has succeeded in spreading the virus of fear into your system.

Fear will not be your portion in Jesus' name. If the devil has the power to kill you during childbirth, he wouldn't tell you, would he? But because he can't do that, he now wants you to agree with him by negotiations. But God has a question for you: "Shall I cause to bring forth, and shut the womb?" (Isa 66:9). Don't make a victim out of yourself. You are not like the other women. You are not permitted to suffer what they suffer. Your rock is the Lord, so do not fear nor be afraid (Deut. 32:31; Isa. 8:12).

You are a special breed, bought with a most costly price: the precious blood of Jesus. You are baptized into the spirit of life. The law of the spirit of life in Christ Jesus is working most mightily in you (Rom. 8: 2). This power is called Zoë, the power of an endless life. God's special favor for safe, sound, and swift delivery is already upon you.

On the day I took my wife to the hospital for delivery, right as we drove through the gate, the devil said to me: Your wife and your baby will not cross this gate alive. I replied and said to him: You will stand at this gate watching as I carry my wife and baby back across this gate alive. I didn't just leave it at that. I went to war to enforce my rights and privileges in the kingdom. I knew that the devil wasn't just making an empty threat. I also knew that if I were to stand strong on God's purpose for my wife and baby, God would bring glory to Himself by making the devil's threat to no effect. All hell was let loose on my wife. The nurses made all the mistakes in the book. She was over-medicated to the point of dizziness. Finally, on the day of delivery, the skies went black with stormy rainfall, lightning, and thunder. They had to brave the aggressive weather conditions to go and fetch the chief medical officer with an ambulance. Meanwhile, I saw the senior nurses who were checking for my baby's fetal beat shake their heads in disappointment with confusion written all over their faces. None of these things moved me into fear because I had already obtained the victory. I was strongly persuaded that God could not fail!!!

Shalom, our first baby, was born looking very dark due to lack of adequate oxygen. He remained in the womb long after the amniotic fluid had burst. My wife lived because God claimed power over her life (Eze. 16:6). He overthrew the counsel of the wicked and gave us the victory.

Why am I sharing this with you? Just to let you know that God will not spare any effort in pulling you through and establishing His purpose in your life if you will place your implicit confidence and faith in Him. God is faithful!

If your mind will stay on God's faithfulness, you will access His perfect peace and everlasting strength (Isa. 26:3-4). This you do by meditating on the word of God as touching your safe delivery every day and all the time.

Fear is trust in the ability of the devil!

Faith is trust in the ability of God!

God has given each one of His sheep eternal life and a promise to ensure their safety. No man can pluck them from His hand! (Jn. 10:27-29).

Case dismissed! You are designed for life. You and your

baby are safe and sound, surrounded by a cloud of glory.

The choice of who to trust is now all yours.

Never allow the devil to terrify you again with the fear of death, for the author of life lives on your inside and the devil knows that. He roars like the lion, but he is not the lion. The real lion of the tribe of Judah lives on your inside. If you will trust Him completely, He will roar against whatever that roars against your safe delivery.

17 CONVENANT OF SAFE DELIVERY

Shall I bring to the birth and not cause to bring forth? (Isa 66:9)

One of the worst fears of most women is the labor room, but in God's agenda, the labor room is designed to be your favor room. In the above text, God asks His people if they truly believe that He would bring them through all the months of their pregnancies all to abandon them at the end. He that gives power to conceive (Heb. 11:11) also gives power to deliver (Isa. 66:9). In other words, He will perfect that which He has started. He is committed to it (Ps. 138:8).

You are more privileged than the Hebrew women. Since their deliveries were spectacular and glorious, yours shall be better because we are under a better covenant (Ex. 1:19). The God who did not abandon the Hebrew women in the hour of their deliveries will be right there to perfect your testimony.

Stop feeding your mind on the fear of what happened to others. It's not permitted to happen to you. If you replace fear with faith in the word of God, you shall have a glorious delivery. Learn to meditate on the truth of the word of God and not on old wives' fables. From conception to delivery, God said that you are licensed to be lively and not sickly. So, think and act lively even when your body is saying otherwise. It's not written anywhere in the bible that 'Thou shalt have morning sicknesses during your seasons of pregnancy.' No. The bible says you shall be lively.

God is personally involved in your delivery! Every other staff in that room, including your doctors, are merely assistants and support staff. The doctor of doctors is the one that has power to put the baby in the womb and will bring the baby out at birth and, of course, He is your God. He is the one whom we call Abba father.

You shall not stay long in that labor room before you come out with your baby (Hos. 13:13). Get your mind renewed with the word of God on these covenant provisions. Write them on your heart! (Prov. 3:3). You are a covenant child of God. Think, talk, and act like you are. Your safe, sound, and swift delivery is part and parcel of God's covenant provisions for you.

Scripture claims in 1 Timothy 2:15 that, "she shall be saved in childbearing, if they continue in faith and charity and holiness with sobriety." Can the scripture be any clearer than this on this matter? You shall be saved in childbearing! Don't give in to fear. When it comes, fight it with the truth of the word of God. God's word concerning you is superior to your feelings. Those tormenting thoughts of death are only a strategy of the devil to create fear in you. You and yours shall live in health to declare the glory of the Lord in the land of the living.

The Almighty God who has said that your oxen may be strong to labor will be right there with you in the labor room to make you stronger, especially now that the church is in the era of painless delivery (Ps. 144:14). Testimonies now abound of covenant women who have stepped into this glorious realm of giving birth without experiencing any form of pain or complications.

In the course of your pregnancy, keep laying your hands

on the baby and decree that the baby must assume its proper place in the womb. Speak to your baby with the voice of faith.

Your baby hears you.

The power of God follows your statements of faith.

Decree that your baby is perfect, proper, and healthy, that your baby is incubating in the power and the presence of the Holy Ghost. Decree that your baby is a marvelous work of God that is powerfully and wonderfully made, that all your baby's pieces are all written in God's book and are perfect and precious in His sight. (Ps 139:13-18).

Your delivery shall be swift, safe and sound in Jesus' precious name. Be confident of this: "He who began a good work in you will complete it until the day of Jesus Christ" (Phil. 1:6).

Confession

I am a covenant daughter of God carrying a covenant child destined to be born supernaturally. I shall give birth like the Hebrew women, for I am lively. I am full of strength by the Holy Ghost. I have the life of God in me. I am supernaturally imparted for speed in delivery.

I speak to my baby and tell it: "You are perfect." I speak to my body: "When the time comes for delivery, you shall fully cooperate with the passage of my baby." My body is the temple of the Holy Spirit. He that lives on my inside is the great One, and He shall cause my baby to come out from the inside to the outside successfully in Jesus' name.

The atmosphere around my labor room shall be controlled, directed, and saturated by the spirit of God. My successful delivery has been ordained in heaven and shall be celebrated here on earth to the glory and praise of my God.

My baby and I shall emerge victorious in Jesus' precious name. Amen.

18 THE POWER OF PICTURING

And he brought him forth abroad, and said, look now toward heaven and tell the stars, if thou be able to number them: and he said unto him, so shall thy seed be. And he believed in the Lord, and he counted it to him for righteousness (Gen. 15:5-6)

Due to the strategic importance of the power of imagination, we wish to present it in this format. To neglect this part is to neglect something important and profound. You need to be a little bit radical with your faith in line with the word of God. When God's time came for Isaac to be born, He gave Abraham a picture to behold. One night, He brought the patriarch outside when the skies were filled up with all kinds of stars and asked him to look up and gaze on them.

God gave him a picture to boost his faith. Each night, Abraham would come out to behold the faces of his children in those stars. He could see Isaac, Jacob, the twelve patriarchs, the entire nation of Israel and, of course, you and me, who are his offspring by faith in the Lord Jesus. He would smile and, later on, retire to his bed, satisfied that the pictures of his descendants that were represented in the sky by the stars are real. He believed God, and He recorded it for him as righteousness. Sometime later, Isaac, the son of promise, was born.

God speaks in terms of pictures. When He was ready to deliver Israel from the house of bondage in Egypt, He gave them the picture of a land flowing with milk and honey. As long as they retained that picture in their hearts, Egypt lost its attraction to them. They were all filled with the desire to get up from the house of bondage and enter into this land of promise. God speaks in terms of pictures, and it works wonders.

Wisdom demands that we follow a time-tested principle in order to reap the benefits therein. The bible, though, demands that we be not lazy but be "followers of them who through faith and patience inherit the promises" (Heb. 6:12).

Some years back, when this truth dawned on me, I made a newspaper cutting of newly born babies and, for a very long time, they were my close companions. If they were not in my bible, then they would be in my diary. Hardly will a day pass by without my seeing them. I wrote some verses of the bible on one of them, which depicted what my faith was expecting. Up until after the yoke of childlessness was broken, those pictures were still with me as evidence that the word of God works. I was following Jeremiah 1:2: "Then said the Lord unto me, thou has well seen. For I will hasten my word to perform it." Do you see the connection between seeing well and God hastening His word? You don't operate faith in a vacuum. Give substance to your faith.

God will ask you what you see (Jer. 1:11). Do you see yourself fruitful? Then keep a literal picture of your dream baby permanently before you. By the way, what prevents you from acting pregnant and taking pictures of yourself in maternity gowns to keep as an image before you? Very soon, it will no longer be acting; it shall be a reality. Faith does and says things that look and sound ridiculous to ordinary people who are not operating from the same spiritual frequency.

The practice of faith is a very serious business that must be undertaken with every fiber of your being. People kept asking me if my wife had taken in, and I kept answering them in the affirmative. Some waited more than nine months to see progress and were disappointed. While they were looking at my wife's womb, I was looking to the word of God that says, "What things soever ye desire, when ye pray, believe that ye receive them, and ye shall have them" (Mk. 11:24).

They were disappointed while I was renewed. We were looking at two different pictures. They were looking out for a physical sign while I had already seen, believed, and received in the invisible. When they finally saw my wife's womb protruding and began to rejoice, I knew they were too late.

Your pictures are powerful enough to deliver results. What you see on the inside, substantiated with a corresponding picture on the outside and a declaration of faith, is a mighty weapon in the quest for your miracle. Don't just give this truth a mental accent; take practical steps of faith that will guarantee your miracle. I see you rejoicing.

19 WARRING WITH PRAISE

He staggered not at the promise of God through unbelief, but was strong in faith giving glory to God (Rom. 4:20)

Praise is the only authentic evidence of a faithful life. It is the expression of our absolute confidence in the ability and faithfulness of God. Abraham took certain steps before he could break the yoke of childlessness in his home. He was surrounded with impossibilities. The doctors' reports were against his expectation of a covenant son and, biologically, he was a write-off, as he and his wife were "old and well stricken with age; and it ceased to be with Sarah after the manner of women" (Gen. 18:11). Even so, he believed that God's word concerning his expectation was superior to the negative situations surrounding him. Against hope, he believed in hope (Rom. 4:18).

Faith fails when we lack a working knowledge of the word of God. Faith fails when we concentrate on the negatives that the eyes can see, especially the medical reports. Doctors' reports, family medical history, old wives' fables, and personal mistakes in life as a result of youthful exuberances are not superior to God's report. Faith fails when we dwell on negative thought patterns instead of meditating on what God has said to us. You shall no longer be weak in faith (Rom. 4:19)! Go to the brookeside of the word of God and, like David, pick up your own stones of the word of faith with which to bring down the Goliath of childlessness. I see you winning.

Abraham deliberately refused to pay attention or spare thought for the negative reports of his biological system (Rom. 4:19). He had lost the power of erection – his own body now dead. His reproductive organ had gone on permanent retirement, but God's power had not. Abraham was about a hundred years old, but God's mercies are new every morning. Sarah's womb was dead, but the word of promise is still alive. Abraham bluntly refused to consider these biological limitations. Their reproductive organs had expired, but they were inspired by the word of faith, which is the womb of all creation. Are you considering God's word or something else? God's word is the reason for our fruitfulness.

Abraham was "strong in faith, giving glory to God" (Rom. 4:20). The most powerful demonstration of his faith in God is captured in that phrase. The day you start praising God excitedly for your children, as though they are already with you, will mark the turning point in your life. Call your baby by name and joyfully thank God for them. By so doing, you are supplying God the raw materials necessary for the perfection of your testimony. The walls of childlessness will be broken as you engage the gear of praise. When you arrive at the place of heartfelt praise, then your miracle is in place. Sing and dance your way to your miracle. Sing heartfelt praises!

Congratulations!!!

20 SCRIPTURAL CONFESSION FOR SUPERNATURAL CONCEPTION (FOR MOTHERS)

Say unto them, as truly as I live, saith the LORD, as you have spoken in my ears, so will I do to you (Num. 14:28)

We having the same spirit of faith, according as it is written, I believed, and therefore have I spoken; we also believe, and therefore speak (2 Cor. 4:13)

Father, I thank you because I have received strength to conceive seed and I shall be delivered of my baby according to your word (Heb. 11:11)

I am a fruitful vine. Children are the heritage from the Lord and the fruit of the womb is his reward (Ps. 127:3)

In my life, as touching my babies, the scriptures cannot be broken. The Lord that says withhold not good from whom it is due when it is in the power of thine hand to do it cannot break His word on me (Prov. 3:27)

God has qualified me for His blessings by imputing the righteousness of Christ upon me. I cannot be denied.

My body as the temple of the Holy Ghost must be obedient to the will of God in my life as touching my baby.

I speak to my reproductive system and tell it to line up with the word of God in the name of Jesus. I command my system to wake up to its functions. I tell my womb, the ovaries, and the fallopian tubes to line up with the word of God now in the name of Jesus.

My womb is forbidden from casting its young in the name of Jesus! Underneath the fruit of my womb is the everlasting hand of the Almighty.

I am a joyful mother of children. I receive the engrafted word of God into my Life now.

I thank you father for your word is true in my life. I thank you for the power to conceive which you have given to me. I thank you for the ability to carry my baby in my womb. I thank you father for nurturing my baby in my womb. I thank you, for my baby is fearfully and wonderfully made. I thank you father for perfectly forming my child's inward parts and knitting my baby together in my womb. All the days of my baby's life are written in your book before they take place or even the substance was formed (Ps. 139:13-16).

Thank you my father for putting joy and laughter into my life, for my baby is good and perfect because every good and perfect gift comes down from you my father (Jm. 1:17).

The Holy Spirit is brooding upon me now and I am prepared for my baby.

I thank you father for making me a joyful mother of babies in Jesus' name. Amen.

21 DESTINY-MOULDING SCRIPTURAL CONFESSIONS FOR EXPECTANT MOTHERS

Today, by the Spirit of faith and prophecy, I declare that the baby I'm carrying is a proper child (Heb. 11: 23)

The Holy Ghost is upon me, and the power of the highest has overshadowed me. This holy child whom I now carry shall be called great (Lk. 1:32-35)

By scriptural prescription and divine ordination, my baby shall be better than the best. You shall be brought into tender favor. God shall give you knowledge and skill in all learning and wisdom and you shall have godly understanding to unravel mysteries. Kings shall commune with you and, in all matters of wisdom and understanding inquired of you, you shall be found ten times better than the best (Dan. 1:9, 17-20).

I dedicate you, my precious baby, unto God (I Sam. 1:11). The spirit of God shall be in, with, and upon you. You shall possess an excellent spirit. Your mind shall be filled with divine knowledge and understanding. You shall be a person of vision (Dan. 5:11-12).

You are a special child, the worthwhile desire of every parent. The blood of Jesus protects your destiny. You shall fulfill your God-ordained purpose in life. Your destiny shall neither be aborted nor truncated. The heart of the Almighty shall thoroughly rejoice for your sake. You shall be the custodian of the secret of the Lord and He will show you His covenant (Ps. 25:14). God shall preserve you.

You shall bring joy to our family and to your generation. Your coming shall mark the dawn of greatness.

Thank you father for this precious gift of yours in Jesus' name.

22 CONFESSIONS FOR SUPERNATURAL CONCEPTION AND CHILDBIRTH

Pastor [Mrs.] Bamigboye of Living Faith Ministries, Winners Chapel, stood on these confessions, despite having a serious problem with her fallopian tubes. Her condition was so serious that it was medically impossible for her to conceive. Today, she and her husband have two wonderful children. It's now your turn for a miracle.

I worship the Lord my God His blessings are upon my food and water. He's taken sickness from me. I will not miscarry nor be barren, and the number of my days He will fulfill (Ex. 23:25-26).

God, my father, help me and in the name of Jesus. I receive His entire blessing for me, those of heaven above, those of the deep, blessings of the breasts and of the womb (Gen. 49:25).

Thus saith the Lord my Redeemer, He that formed me from the womb: "I am the Lord that maketh all things." Praise the Lord; God is perfectly forming my healthy baby in my womb. Jesus defeated Satan, and the enemy cannot touch my body. The Lord stretched out the heavens alone and spread abroad the earth and His ways of creation are perfect. I will only accept God's perfection concerning my baby and in the functioning of my body (Isa. 46:24).

The Lord that carried me from the womb shall also carry my baby from my womb at the appointed time, for God has formed my baby and keeps watch over him (Isa. 46:3-4).

Father, children are your heritage and the fruit of the womb your reward. While this child is yet forming in my womb, I dedicate him unto you in the name of Jesus. I thank you that my baby is in your hands and the wicked one toucheth him not, for he is shielded about with the name of Jesus (Ps. 127:3).

All my children shall be thought of the Lord and great shall be their peace (Isa. 54:13).

Lord, you have upheld me from the time of my birth; you brought me from my mother's womb at your appointed hour. I thank you that you shall also bring forth my baby at your perfect hour. I praise thee continually (Ps. 71:6).

I meditate on the word of God and keep it before mine eyes. The Lord loves me, blesses me, and multiplies me. He has blessed the fruit of my womb and all that I need each day to live in abundance. I stand on the word of God that says I shall never be barren, and Jesus Christ has taken all my sicknesses from me (Deut. 7:13-15).

No pain or suffering accompanies my labor or delivery; I refuse to accept in Jesus' name, and my offspring will be with me forever in Jesus' name (Isa. 66:7).

The Lord maketh the barren woman to keep house and to be the joyful mother of children (Ps. 113:9). Praise ye the Lord!

Pain in childbirth is under the curse and Christ has been made a curse for us that we should walk in the redemption He provided for us. Therefore, I refuse to accept any pain or complication during my pregnancy and delivery (Gen. 3:16; Gal. 3:26).

Father, I thank you that you perfectly form my child's inward parts and knit him together in my womb. I praise thee, for the creation of my baby is wonderful. All the days of his life are written in your book before they take place or even his substance was formed (Ps. 139:13-16; 1 Tim. 2:15; Isa. 54:17; Num. 23:23).

Lord, I thank you that you feed your flock and are gathering and carrying your lambs in your bosom and gently leading and directing those with young (Isa. 40:11).

My baby is good and perfect, for every good and perfect gift cometh

down from my father above (Jm. 1:17).
      In Jesus' name (Amen)

Write and sign your name on the dotted line. By so doing, you are personalizing these confessions.

23 SCRIPTURAL CONFESSION FOR FATHERS

Father, I thank you, for my body is the temple of the Holy Spirit (1 Cor. 6:19)

I am complete in Christ who is the head of all principalities and power (Col. 2:10)

My seed shall be mighty upon the earth (Ps. 112:2). I and the children whom the Lord shall give to me are for signs and wonders (Isa. 8:18)

My sons shall be as plants grown up in their youth while my daughters shall be as corner stones polished after the similitude of a palace (Ps. 114:12.

I am a very fruitful vine, for as arrows are in the hand of a mighty man, so shall be my children. I am a happy man because I have my quiver full of them for children are my heritage from my God (Ps. 127:3-5)

I speak to my reproductive system to be obedient to the word of God. Since everything produces after its kind, my entire system must be obedient to the eternal decree of the Almighty that says: be fruitful and multiply (Gen. 1:24, 27,-28)

I command my sperm and the entire reproductive system to line up now with the word of God in Jesus' name! My faith has touched my children, and I shall have them, for with God, nothing shall be impossible (Mk. 11:24; Lk. 1:37).

I am a living proof that my God is faithful and cannot break His word on my covenant child (Ps. 89:34-35). This I know, for the scriptures cannot be broken (Jn. 10:35).

Everything obeys the law of faith, so I call forth my desired child now, for this is the confidence that I have in my God. If I ask anything according to His will, He will hear me, and I know that I have obtained the petition that I desired of Him (1 Jn. 5:14-15).

I give God praise for my children in Jesus' name. Amen

24 GOD HAS NOT FINISHED WITH YOU
(BY DOROTHY, MY WIFE)

If your case is the same with mine or close to it or worse than it, I wish to let you know that God has not finished with you. When we were first married, we desired a child and, as the days turn to weeks and the weeks to months and the months became years, this desire started to feel far-fetched, until it finally dawned on us that life is a battleground. We are already victorious in Christ. If you must win, you must apply the winning principles outlined in this book.

Was it fun to contest and have that which was my right from God? NO!

Did we cry? Yes.

Were we sometimes discouraged? Yes.

But the miracle came when I quit worrying.

I wish to share with you the story of Hermie and Wormie. Both were caterpillars destined to be butterflies, but they never knew this and they became so worried and envious of every other creature. They questioned God. But later, they metamorphosed into butterflies when they stopped worrying.

The bible says: Man that is in honor and knows it not is like the beast that perishes (Psalm 49:20). You have the honor of having your child if that is your desire.

This was close to my testimony. Shalom came the year I stopped worrying and rested in God. As you stop worrying and become trustful, the Lord will hear and honor you. Amen.

-Dorothy

25 JUST FOR YOU

The last chapter of this book will be written with your testimonies. As God performs your miracles, please share them with us with pictures of your baby/babies .

Your testimonies will form the sequel to this book, which will be entitled, "Testimonies of Covenant Childbirth".

We dedicate this book to the joy of families all across the continents of the earth.

May your joy be full in Jesus' name. Out of your loins and bosoms shall come forth males and females who shall be mighty upon this earth to the glory of our great and mighty God in Jesus' Name. Amen.

POSTSCRIPT

The LORD makes the barren woman
To keep house and to be a joyful
Mother of children, praise ye the lord (Ps. 113:9)
For with God nothing shall be impossible (Lk 1:37)

COVENANT CHILDBIRTH PRAYER CONFERENCES

To participate in the next covenant childbirth prayer conference, call the numbers below for the date, time, venue, and seat reservation.

Experience God's power in a most unusual way as you receive the miracle touch of the Holy Ghost.

Experience the power of divine breakthrough in our next meeting.

You cannot be denied for we have access by the blood Jesus.

+234 817 751 8684
+234 816 358 8989
+234 805 488 4696,

covenantchildbirth@gmail.com

ABOUT THE AUTHOR

Callistus Ike is the pastor of Christ for All Mission Inc. He holds a B.S. degree in Sociology, a diploma from Word of Faith Bible Institute, and certificate from DayStar Leadership Academy. He speaks in Conferences and Seminars. He is married to his wife Dorothy and their marriage is blessed with three wonderful children. His passion in life is to make Christ known. Pastor Callistus has trained many church leaders in the art of Church management through his Leadership Training program.

EDITOR'S NOTE

This book qualifies for the publisher's One-for-One Challenge. Buy a copy, and publisher will donate $1 dollar to establish resource centers for orphanages in developing countries, where these amazing kids may learn to read, dream, and grow. Just because they are orphans doesn't mean their future has to be limited. Learn more at www.kharispublishing.com.

As a social enterprise, Kharis Publishing has a two-fold mission: giving voice to underrepresented authors (including women, minorities, internationals, and first-time authors) to publish their books free of charge; and empowering orphans through literacy initiatives. Kharis Publishing also welcomes corporate partnerships with churches, libraries, and schools.